Israel's Destiny

Israel's Destiny

by
S. Maxwell Coder

MOODY PRESS
CHICAGO

© 1978 by
THE MOODY BIBLE INSTITUTE
OF CHICAGO

Cover photo courtesy AV Department Library, MBI

Library of Congress Cataloging in Publication Data

Coder, Samuel Maxwell, 1902-
 Israel's destiny.

 Includes bibliographical references.
 1. Bible—Prophecies—Jews. 2. Bible—Prophecies—
Palestine. I. Title.
BS649.J5C58   220.1'5   78-9659
ISBN 0-8024-4182-3

Printed in the United States of America

Contents

Contents

Foreword

It has long been my privilege to have Jewish friends who worship God according to the teachings of Judaism while they await the coming of their Messiah. They do not agree with me that Jesus of Nazareth, my Savior and Lord, is also the true Messiah of Israel. When we have discussed our differences in the light of the Scriptures, they have always shown the utmost kindness and consideration.

I hope these friends and other Jewish people who read this book will realize that I cannot but speak of the deepest convictions of my own heart as I write about the destiny of Israel. In any case, here is a statement of what the Dean of Education Emeritus of Moody Bible Institute understands the Bible to teach about the future of the Jewish people, the land of Palestine, and the city of Jerusalem. It has been written after a lifetime of study, teaching, and discussion with other evangelical Christians who know and love the Scriptures.

Introduction

Israel's destiny is a major theme of Scripture, which describes a glorious future for the people, their land, and their capital, Jerusalem. It is surprising that Bible encyclopedias and dictionaries have very little to say about the subject, and no work dealing with this wonderful theme seems to be available. After waiting in vain for someone else to assemble in brief and orderly fashion this truly remarkable revelation, I have put together in book form my own study notes.

To judge by the surprise and pleasure exhibited by audiences everywhere, even in the city of Jerusalem itself, when addresses have been given on what the Bible declares to be the future of the Jewish people and the Holy Land, there is widespread interest today in what is going to happen.

The purpose of this book is to examine the actual words written by Israel's prophets without speculating on what they may have meant but did not say. This is being "literalistic," of course, but I believe God holds us responsible for what is written in His Word rather than for our ability to find hidden meanings in it. It is exciting to take the text of the Bible as it stands, accepting the plain, ordinary sense of the language, with a minimum of scholarly help in tracing the primary meanings of some of the original Hebrew words. It leads to the discovery that the prophets have given us a surprisingly clear, complete, and detailed picture of the future history and final destiny of Israel.

This brief summary of what the Scriptures actually say is intended for Jewish people and Christians who may not have had the opportunity to examine Bible prophecy with care, as well as others who belong to neither of these categories. A complete divine program is stated in Scripture, with Israel at the heart of it. It has not been easy to select representative passages about such a vast subject. No attempt has been made to incorporate the extensive material on Messianic prophecy. What is found in this book is the substance of a course of study taught at Moody Bible Institute and given at various Bible conferences in America and elsewhere.

THE PEOPLE OF ISRAEL

1

A Remarkable People

There is nothing more fascinating in all literature than the Bible revelation of the destiny of Israel, the only nation whose history was written in advance. It is not generally known that it was Moses who gave us the first complete outline of what is going to happen to the Jewish people (Deut. 28:1—30:10). It extends from the occupation of the land of Palestine by Israel all the way to the coming of the Messiah to rule over His glorious kingdom during earth's golden age. A score of other prophets have filled in countless details. Everything fits together in a mosaic so extraordinary as to confound the human intellect and lead to the conclusion that such a record demands a supernatural explanation.

Much of what was written has already taken place. The stage seems to be set for climactic events yet to come. For the proper understanding of all this, some knowledge is needed of a few elementary facts about the strange people called the Jews some three hundred times in Scripture. They are the only nation made up of one family. All are descended from one

man. They are children of Abraham and Isaac, sons
and daughters of the patriarch Jacob, who became
Israel. Their genealogy is carefully recorded in the
Bible.

They bear a portrait four thousand years old.
Characteristics found in the Hebrews of olden times
reappear today. There are even physical re-
semblances. The likeness of Jehu on the Black
Obelisk in the British Museum is unmistakably
Jewish. Men who look like him can be seen
everywhere today, although it is often difficult to dis-
tinguish by appearance only between Jewish people
and those among whom they live.

The Hebrews have been the most persecuted
people in history. There is even a word to describe it:
anti-Semitism. Much has been written about its possible causes. Scholars have offered explanations
based on economic, religious, and even personal
factors. The true explanation is to be found in the
Bible, and it is supernatural.

An examination of the Scriptures shows anti-
Semitism to be one of the results rising from the
relationship between the people of Israel and their
God. An invisible war is going on between the God of
the Bible and the unseen world of evil spirits. Beginning at the dawn of history, it ultimately became
focused on Israel, the ancient, chosen people of God.

The ruler of the wicked hosts of darkness who
opposes God and His people is called Satan in fifty-
five texts of Scripture. He is given various names and
titles in twenty-three different books. Described as
the wisest and most attractive created being in the
universe, he is the god and prince of this present, evil
world (Ezek. 28:12-19; John 14:30; 2 Cor. 4:4),

leader of an innumerable company of fallen angels. He is the great deceiver of the nations (Rev. 12:9) whose unseen influence is behind attitudes and actions on their part that would otherwise be inexplicable.

This fearsome being hates the Jews. For thousands of years he has sought to destroy them. He is aware that God said to them, "Thou art an holy people unto the LORD thy God: the LORD thy God hath chosen thee to be a special people unto himself, above all people that are upon the face of the earth" (Deut. 7:6). He knows it was God's purpose to give the Bible to the world through this people, and eventually the Seed of the woman who was destined to bruise the head of the old serpent, Satan, as God announced in the Garden of Eden (Gen. 3:15).

Some passages of Scripture having to do with the important place given to Israel in the divine program for the human race are rejected by a few as simply incredible. Among these are the words appearing in the song of Moses, "When the Most High divided to the nations their inheritance, when he separated the sons of Adam, he set the bounds of the people according to the number of the children of Israel" (Deut. 32:8). Whether or not we comprehend fully the meaning of this revelation, it is one of the great clues to history. The size of the nations of the world was, or is, somehow related to the size of the world's population of Jews. Somewhere behind the growth of Gentile nations and their military conquests stands this divine disclosure.

The ferocity of Satan's attacks on the Jewish people can be seen again and again in Scripture. It is found in ancient Egypt when Pharaoh gave orders to have every male child killed (Exod. 1:16). After it was revealed that the Messiah was to come through the descendants of King David, all of the royal seed were destroyed on three separate occasions except for a single individual (2 Chron. 21:4; 21:17; 22:1, 10-12). At one time, all the divine promises of a coming deliverer were dependent on the life of one six-year-old prince, hidden away by the priests in the temple for six years after all others in the Messianic line had been killed. During the captivity in Medo-Persia in the days of Ahasuerus, satanic hatred was seen again in Haman's attempt to destroy the entire nation (Esther 3:6).

Christians believe they see the continuation of this devilish attack in Herod's attempt on the life of Jesus of Nazareth when He was a baby and in other efforts to destroy Him, culminating in the crucifixion. The remarkable statement is made in the New Testament that if the princes of this world had understood the inscrutable purposes of God, "they would not have crucified the Lord of glory" (1 Cor. 2:8). Unperceived by Satan at the time, the crucifixion became the means of his defeat.

The Jews are remarkable for their antiquity. Their history goes back to about 2000 B.C. Other nations are young by comparison. The people of Israel have seen empires rise, come to great power, decay, and die, and they have attended their funerals. We may think of the Roman Empire as ancient, but the city of Rome was a village of huts on the bank of the Tiber when, in the year 555 B.C., Daniel was in Babylon writing about the future of the empire. Even at that time, Israel had been a nation for 450 years.

The early literature of the Jews offers details of

great interest. God gave His chosen people power to get wealth (Deut. 8:18), an ability they have never lost. He gave them wisdom. Solomon was the wisest mortal who ever lived. Daniel stood so far above the most brilliant men of Babylon that he was promoted by King Nebuchadnezzar to be "ruler over the whole province of Babylon" (Dan. 2:48). In our own time there is a disproportionately large number of Jews in every important profession requiring wisdom and skill. Ever since they were dispersed among the nations, they have given outstanding leadership wherever they have gone. They are prominent in science, medicine, art, literature, music, business, and industry.

The Bible, given to the world by Jewish hands, is so superior to every other book that it still stands alone after thousands of years. It contains the answer to every problem of the human heart. The laws of civilized nations are based on its Ten Commandments. The eclipse of this Book would plunge the world into chaos; its extinction would be the epitaph of history.

Long ago it was said about the Hebrews, "The people shall dwell alone, and shall not be reckoned among the nations" (Num. 23:9). No better capsule description could be written. The Jews have always been a people set apart from all others. Their determination to preserve their culture and religion has made them prefer to live by themselves, resisting amalgamation with the nations in which they have settled. Their Sabbath and holidays have also set them apart. Sometimes anti-Semitism has helped to preserve them by confining them to ghettos. Even when they are free, they tend to associate with one another.

Every other nation looks back into history to find its finest hour, but Israel's golden age is still future. Prophecies without number describe their coming kingdom under the Messiah. Those beautiful descriptions of a society unlike anything ever known on earth are not taken seriously by many of the people who are aware of their existence. However, a glorious future kingdom is not the end of the story. The Bible carries the inspired record of the future of the Jews on into eternity. The promise of God to Israel is: "As the new heavens and the new earth, which I will make, shall remain before me, saith the LORD, so shall your seed and your name remain" (Isa. 66:22).

The very fabric of Scripture emphasizes the importance of this people. The story of the entire human race, from Adam to the call of Abram, is covered in the short space of the first eleven chapters of the book of Genesis. It extends over a period of two thousand years, according to some calculations. By contrast, four-fifths of the Bible is devoted to the people of Israel during the following two thousand years. Only one-fifth of its pages is given to the divine program concerning the church, which curiously has also been in existence for two thousand years.

These three periods total six thousand years, according to popular chronology. This fact has special interest today because there is an ancient Jewish tradition that says human history is to continue for 6,000 years before Israel's kingdom brings 1,000 years of peace and prosperity. Those who believe the tradition has merit see parallels between this division of time into 6,000 years and 1,000 years, the record of creation, in which six days were followed by a seventh day of rest, and the commemorative six-day week followed by a Sabbath.

(The people of Israel provide the true key to history. God's purpose for the human race is centered in His chosen people.) When conditions in the world approach those described in Scripture for the last days of Israel, the end of Gentile world government will be near. The rebirth of national life among the Jews means the dawn is in the sky for them after a long night of war, suffering, hunger, disease, and death extending over the many centuries of their dispersion. God has announced that He is going to intervene in the affairs of men some day. We can get some idea of when this will be by examining what the Bible says about the people of Israel. No one interested in world events can afford to be ignorant of what God has revealed about them.

Millions today believe the stars forecast the future. They seek to guide their lives by what astrologers tell them to do. Others study the announcements of seers and false prophets, no matter how often such predictions have been discredited. Cult leaders talk of the end of the world and guess when it will come. Standing out amid these uncertain voices and conflicting ideas is the clear testimony of Scripture.

Isaiah wrote the word of the Lord: "I am God, and there is none like me, declaring the end from the beginning, and from ancient times the things that are not yet done, saying, My counsel shall stand, and I will do all my pleasure" (Isa. 46:9-10). The unfolding divine program is set forth by the Hebrew prophets with remarkable clarity and completeness. It is possible to write out this program in language anyone can understand, supporting every statement with a reference to its source in the Bible. God has given us a plain and trustworthy description of the destiny of Israel, the nations, and the world. To this the New Testament adds the glorious destiny of the church. Each of these great prophetic themes is worthy of careful study. So many details are given to each that in our examination of what has been written about Israel, only passing reference to other subjects is possible. (It is the ancient, chosen people who bind together every prophetic subject having to do with this world and the world to come.)

2

The Great Prophecy of Moses

At the outset of any study of the vast body of Bible truth about Israel's destiny, it should be emphasized that such an exercise is not possible with any other literature in the entire world, from any country, at any age. (True prophecy of coming events is found only in Scripture.) Occasionally the media feature currently popular mystics, astrologers, and others who claim to be able to see into the future. One remarkable trait characterizes such individuals: they speak in glowing terms about successes they profess to have had in the past, but when asked about coming events they avoid plain statements in favor of obscure generalities.

Our wisest leaders are unable to predict what is going to happen in the next month or year in any field of interest. If among the uncounted thousands of volumes written by brilliant men and women in past centuries a single phrase is found that can be claimed as a true example of accurate forecasting, it is seized upon and quoted as proof that prophecy is to be found somewhere else than in the Bible.

The outstanding example of such a phrase from ancient literature is a statement from Seneca, the Roman philosopher credited with a prediction of the discovery of America by Columbus. It is the only sentence most people have ever heard of from his pen. At a time when Strabo and others suspected the existence of new continents in the vast, unexplored areas of the world, Seneca hazarded the guess, "There shall come a time in later ages, when ocean shall relax its chains and a vast continent appear, and a pilot shall find new worlds." He said nothing to identify America or Columbus, but his words are treated with reverence not accorded to the writers of the Bible, as though such a conjecture made him a remarkable prophet.

The Word of God contains hundreds of clear and specific prophecies written centuries before the events took place. History has recorded the fulfillment of many such prophecies dealing with nations, cities, individuals, climatic conditions, the economy, wars, famines, pestilence, migrations, enslavement, and great deliverances. Precise details are often given in unambiguous language, with names and time periods stated in unmistakable terms. If the language of prophecy is sometimes obscure, however, we are informed that it is intentionally so. When Daniel was curious about something he himself had written at the command of a divine messenger, he was told, "The words are closed up and sealed till the time of the end" (Dan. 12:9).

The prophets present an orderly, progressive outline of the history of the Jews from their beginnings until their final destiny. Since this fact is well known, efforts have sometimes been made to escape the plainness of the language by claims that the text does not actually mean what it says, or that it is a kind of pious fraud. Some who reject the literal meaning of what the prophets have written insist on spiritualizing the text, or allegorizing it, in an effort to find some hidden meaning at variance with the ordinary meaning of the words. Even these critics must begin with what is written, of course. It is our purpose not only to begin with what is written, but to limit ourselves to the words found in the Bible. They can plead their own case as to whether they are worthy of the consideration of intelligent people. We need not depart from the normal sense of the words chosen by the writers. Nor need we be concerned with passages admittedly difficult to understand. There is an abundance of truth stated in unequivocal terms.

The best way to begin the adventure of exploring the vast body of Bible truth about Israel's destiny is to examine the outline of history revealed to Moses and written by him some thirty-five hundred years ago (Deut. 28:1—30:10). It presents in chronological order many of the great divisions of Jewish history from the beginnings of the Jewish people as a nation until the establishment of Messiah's kingdom. It is the first and most comprehensive of many prophetic outlines to be found throughout the Bible.

Here are the first bold strokes of a divine mural that is expanded and completed by later prophets. Every detail supplied by them throughout succeeding centuries fits perfectly into what Moses wrote. All of it is said to have proceeded from the mind of

God. No human intelligence could have produced such an amazing record of coming events, written many centuries before they took place.

When God gave to Moses an account of what was going to happen to his people during the next several thousand years, the Hebrews had been in the wilderness for thirty-eight years, after escaping from Egypt. Soon they would enter Palestine and conquer the inhabitants under the leadership of Joshua. The first part of the prophecy has to do with their experiences after they gained possession of the land God had promised to them (Deut. 28:1-14). It covers a period of approximately four hundred fifty years.

Moses was told the Jews were going to enjoy the favor of God as long as they obeyed His voice and kept His commandments. They would greatly multiply in the land, and their cattle would increase. Plentiful rain producing abundant crops was promised. The people of Israel were destined to become prosperous. No enemy would be able to stand before them. Leadership among the nations was to be their fortunate lot. Everywhere men would recognize them as the favored people of God.

Everything came to pass as Moses had predicted. The blessing of God rested so wonderfully on His people that they became a great nation, were respected by their neighbors, and enjoyed a series of impressive military victories. Refreshing rains fell. Rich crops of every kind were harvested. Everything the Jews did prospered under the good hand of their God. A considerable part of the early books of the Old Testament, beginning with the book of Joshua, describes the blessings of those years.

The second part of Moses' prophecy describes a drastic change (Deut. 28:15-35). It was to take place only after the Jews turned away from God and rebelled against His commandments. "If thou wilt not hearken unto the voice of the LORD thy God, to observe to do all his commandments and his statutes which I command thee this day; . . . all these curses shall come upon thee, and overtake thee" (Deut. 28:15). There follows a dreadful listing of the divine judgments to come on the people if they sinned against the Lord by turning away from Him.

Again, history brought the fulfillment of the prophecy. Following some four hundred fifty years of blessing between the days of Joshua and the breakup of Solomon's kingdom (covered in fourteen verses of Moses' summary), various judgments culminating in the captivities fell on the nation. Moses devoted twenty-one verses to that period. The divine favor enjoyed for so long was withdrawn. The rains ceased, the heavens became like brass, and the ground became as hard as iron. Pestilence ravaged the people. One military defeat followed another. The Jews fled before their enemies. They lost their homes, vineyards, and cattle. They saw their children taken away to other lands as captives. There were occasional periods of obedience, revival, and blessing, but the apostasy grew steadily worse. Israel was ready for the third period of its history, described by its greatest leader even before they entered their promised land.

Wrote Moses, "The LORD shall bring thee, and thy king which thou shalt set over thee, unto a nation which neither thou nor thy fathers have known; and there shalt thou serve other gods, wood and stone"

(Deut. 28:36). The story of how this was to come about is told in only twenty-seven verses (Deut. 28:36-62). Almost unbelievable tragedies would accompany it. A fierce and cruel nation was to invade Palestine, besiege Israel's fenced cities, destroy the fruit of the land and its cattle, and carry away the population as captives.

Some details of this prophecy might seem impossible of realization if their fulfillments were not later recorded in Scripture and in secular historical documents. "Thou shalt eat the fruit of thine own body, the flesh of thy sons and of thy daughters, which the LORD thy God hath given thee, in the siege, and in the straitness, wherewith thine enemies shall distress thee" (Deut. 28:53). This was to come "because thou servedst not the LORD thy God with joyfulness, and with gladness of heart, for the abundance of all things; therefore shalt thou serve thine enemies which the LORD shall send against thee, in hunger, and in thirst, and in nakedness, and in want of all things" (Deut. 28:47-48).

When the predicted time had come, the Assyrian armies invaded the land and in 721 B.C. deported the northern tribes of Israel as captives (2 Kings 17:1-8). Afterward Nebuchadnezzar led the Babylonian armies against the southern tribes. The people were removed from the land in 586 B.C.; Jerusalem was destroyed (2 Kings 25:1-12).

The fourth part of Moses' prophecy brings us all the way to modern times (Deut. 28:63-68). He passed over a number of important facts about Jewish history, such as the return of some Jews to Palestine to repopulate the land in preparation for the events of the New Testament, predicted by

Jeremiah and described in the books of Ezra and Nehemiah. Instead, he announced the world dispersion of the chosen people that continues to this day. "The Lord shall scatter thee among all people, from the one end of the earth even unto the other. . . . And among these nations shalt thou find no ease, neither shall the sole of thy foot have rest: but the LORD shall give thee there a trembling heart, and failing of eyes, and sorrow of mind" (Deut. 28:64-65).

In the year A.D. 70, Titus led the armies of the Roman Empire against Judea. Fifteen hundred years had now passed since the prophecy of Moses was written. Jerusalem was destroyed and leveled. The people of Israel who survived the attack were sold as slaves throughout the empire. That was nearly two thousand years ago. The Jewish people are still scattered among all nations, although a sufficient number have returned to form a Jewish state in the land of their fathers. Countless times the Jews have had occasion to remember that Moses wrote:

> Thy life shall hang in doubt before thee; and thou shalt fear day and night, and shalt have none assurance of thy life: in the morning thou shalt say, Would God it were even! and at even thou shalt say, Would God it were morning! for the fear of thine heart wherewith thou shalt fear, and for the sight of thine eyes which thou shalt see (Deut. 28:66-67).

The astonishing accuracy of Moses' prophecy has been demonstrated throughout the thirty-five hundred years that have passed since he wrote it. We must therefore take seriously his announcement of a coming fifth period in the unfolding story of the Jews (Deut. 30:1-10). In many respects it transcends even the wonder of their beginnings, when God brought them out of Egypt with miraculous displays of His power. There is no good reason for doubting that what is written in the closing ten verses of the prophecy will be fulfilled as accurately as what is written in the first sixty-eight verses.

Moses began the concluding part of his prophecy with the words,

> And it shall come to pass, when all these things are come upon thee, the blessing and the curse, which I have set before thee, and thou shalt call them to mind among all the nations, whither the LORD thy God hath driven thee, and shalt return unto the LORD thy God, and shalt obey his voice according to all that I command thee this day, thou and thy children, with all thine heart, and with all thy soul (Deut. 30:1-2).

These words, stated so simply, set forth the conditions destined to precede the future intervention of God on behalf of His ancient people. Other prophets develop the theme of those conditions and that intervention. The day is coming when Jewish people all over the world will remember what is written about the blessings they once enjoyed, as well as the long years when the nation experienced "the curse" imposed because of disobedience.

The memory of their priceless heritage and the bitter price the nation has paid for turning away from God is going to have a tremendous effect on Jewish people everywhere. They will return to the Lord and obey His voice in all the commandments Moses gave their forefathers. This will involve their children as well. It will be a serious business, requiring obedience with all their hearts, and all their souls. Not every Jew then living will do this, however. Isaiah indicates that it will be a "remnant," that is, only a part of what is evidently a large population of Jewish people living all over the world at that time (Isa. 10:20-22).

These introductory words describing a change of heart on the part of Jews everywhere at some future time are followed by an important time word, "then." When remembrance of what was written by Moses about the blessing and the curse is followed by a return to the Lord on the part of Jewish people, "then the LORD thy God will turn thy captivity, and have compassion upon thee, and will return and gather thee from all the nations, whither the LORD thy God hath scattered thee" (Deut. 30:3).

A tremendous change is coming to Jewish people all over the world. There will be a return to the Lord and obedience to His Word. Not until this takes place will the closing words of Moses' prophecy be fulfilled. No local awakening is in view; it is something that takes place "among all the nations" where the Jews are scattered. Moses does not tell us what it is that brings about such a transformation in attitude, but other prophets shed light on it.

For example, in an extended passage to be examined in detail later, Ezekiel describes a latter-day invasion of Palestine by great armies from the north (Ezek. 38-39). The wrath of God will be so deeply aroused that He will destroy the invaders in such a manner that the whole world will be apalled. Men everywhere will know God has intervened on behalf of the people of Israel, but the Jews will be particularly impressed. Ezekiel tells us, "The house of Israel shall know that I am the LORD their God from that day and forward" (Ezek. 39:22). Many will be so deeply impressed that they will recall ancient times when God performed miracles for their fathers, and they will turn back to Him with all their being. The hour will have struck for further divine activity.

Nor is this the only indication in Scripture that powerful influences will be at work to shake the descendants of Abraham from their lethargy. The book of Revelation supplies the information that in those same latter days God is to send two witnesses who will prophesy for a period of 1,260 days, arousing such animosity on the part of their enemies that they are finally martyred in the streets of Jerusalem (Rev. 11:3-12). Another passage speaks of the lifting of the blindness divinely imposed on the Jews according to the prophet Isaiah (Isa. 6:9-10; Rom. 11:25). It may also be that the vast literature produced about Israel during the present age will have a powerful impact on the Jews of that day.

Every phrase of this part of the prophecy of Moses deserves careful study. These brief statements are greatly enlarged by other prophets of God. The first promise is "that then the LORD thy God will turn thy captivity" (Deut. 30:3). A Hebrew idiom is used that has nothing to do with a return of captives or the end of the dispersion. It means deliverance from trouble, a return to prosperity after a season of adversity. A similar usage appears in the book of Job. After he had lost his family and property and was afflicted with a terrible disease that covered his body with boils, "the LORD turned the captivity of Job" by restoring his health and prosperity (Job 42:10). An extended time of affliction came to an end.

When God turns the captivity of Israel He will restore to them the enjoyment of their original covenanted mercies and blessings. In the ancient Greek translation of the Old Testament called the Septuagint, the passage is rendered, "The Lord will heal thy sins." Scripture makes it plain that this is not equivalent to what is sometimes called the national conversion of Israel, but it is to be so wonderful a change that it will lead to world-transforming events. It is the first movement in the great symphony of Israel's restoration to the divine favor experienced in Old Testament times. Apart from this return to God and obedience to His word given through Moses, there can be no regathering of the Jews by the returning Lord, and no restoration to the land in fulfillment of prophecy.

It must be remembered that Moses gives in brief outline some of the important future events involving the people of Israel, but not all of them. We know from other prophecies that a dreadful time of world tribulation will find the Jewish people at its center. Satanic hatred and persecution will reach new heights. In the words of Daniel, "there shall be a time of trouble, such as never was since there was a nation even to that same time: and at that time thy people shall be delivered, every one that shall be found written in the book" (Dan. 12:1). All Moses tells us is that after the Lord turns the captivity of His ancient people, He will have compassion on them. There will be a dark period during which they are going to need that compassion.

There can be no escaping the plain meaning of the next phrase in the words of Moses. The King James Version of the Bible and the Holy Scriptures published by the Jewish Publication Society use identical language in declaring, "The LORD thy God . . . will return and gather" the Jews from all the peoples, or nations, where He has scattered them. For Him to return implies a previous departure from the earth.

Everyone who has read the Bible knows the Lord withdrew His presence from His people because of their persistent sin. Several passages mention this. Ezekiel even describes the withdrawing of His glory from the temple and from Jerusalem, which glory manifested His presence among them (Ezek. 10:4, 18, 19; 11:23). Isaiah ties together the departure of the Lord from Israel and His future coming to re-gather them: "For a small moment have I forsaken thee; but with great mercies will I gather thee" (Isa. 54:7). Perhaps the most striking Old Testament passage referring to a departure of the Lord and a later return is found in Hosea 5:15: "I will go and return to my place, till they acknowledge their offence, and seek my face: in their affliction they will seek me early."

Many Jews are aware that Christians believe the return of the Lord of which Moses spoke is identical to the return of Jesus of Nazareth at His second coming to the earth. It is remarkable that the language used by Hosea has in view a particular offense by the people of Israel rather than the general attitude that characterizes the present age. Christians believe it refers to the sin of rejecting the Messiah when He came in the person of Jesus. Matthew

23:39 is looked upon as parallel to Hosea's words: "Ye shall not see me henceforth, till ye shall say, Blessed is he that cometh in the name of the Lord." This passage occurs in the lament over Jerusalem; it was addressed to the Jewish people of that time. There are other time words in passages having to do with Christ's return: "Whom the heaven must receive until the times of restitution of all things, which God hath spoken by the mouth of all his holy prophets since the world began" (Acts 3:21).

The Bible speaks of many things that accompany or follow the return of the Lord. Moses said simply that the Lord "will return and gather thee from all the nations, whither the LORD thy God hath scattered thee." This divine gathering together of Jewish people from all over the world is not to be confused with their later restoration to the land of Palestine. As we learn from Ezekiel, they will be gathered together at a wilderness place, where the rebels and transgressors will be screened out by the Lord (Ezek. 20:34-42). Not until then will He bring His people into their own land. Thus, the regathering and the restoration are two distinct events in the divine program.

The present gathering of many Jews to Palestine from various nations is not the divine regathering and restoration of which Moses wrote. As further study will make clear, the present fragmentary return is anticipated in Scripture, but the great prophecies of the regathering of Israel have to do with the supernatural activity of God after the return of the Lord from heaven, and not before. In Moses' words, "The LORD thy God will bring thee into the land which thy fathers possessed, and thou shalt possess it; and he will do thee good, and multiply thee above thy fathers" (Deut. 30:5).

The concluding words of this remarkable prophetic history of the Jews speak of the kingdom age. At that time the Lord will cause the people to love Him with all their hearts and souls. The curses that rested on them will be placed on their enemies and those who persecuted them. Obedience to God's commandments will be the order of the day. God will respond by making them plenteous in every work of their hands. Children will be born. Cattle will multiply, and crops and orchards will produce abundantly. The Lord will rejoice over His people for good, as He rejoiced over their fathers.

This is as far as Moses carries us in his prophecy of the future of his people. Other prophets take up the story, develop every major theme mentioned in Deuteronomy, fill in the blanks, and trace the future of Israel all the way into eternity. Innumerable details are given about the prosperity and blessing of the Jews during their coming golden age under the Messiah. They will greatly increase in numbers, the size of the land will be enlarged, the curse will be removed in measure, and the city of Jerusalem will be elevated above the surrounding countryside, becoming the joy of the whole earth as the residence of Israel's Messiah and King. Men may refuse to believe what is written, but they cannot deny that the wonderful things we are examining are plainly written in the Scripture of truth.

3

Three Departures
from the Land

About four thousand years ago, after the whole world had turned away from the true God, a man named Terah and his son Abram lived in the Chaldean city of Ur. Like their countrymen, the family had long worshiped pagan gods, but in Abram God found a man willing to listen to Him. He said, "Get thee out of thy country, and from thy kindred, and from thy father's house, unto a land that I will shew thee" (Gen. 12:1; see also Josh. 24:15).

Abram is sometimes called a Gentile, but at that time in history the distinction between Jews and Gentiles did not yet exist. The human race was one. The word *Jew* does not appear in the Bible until the days of the kings of Israel, when it came into use to designate those who had descended from Judah, one of Abram's great-grandsons. Abram was an uncommonly gifted and righteous resident of the land of Chaldea who believed the word he received from God.

Scripture gives a simple and brief statement of the purpose God had in mind when He chose this one man and told him to leave his homeland for a country he had never seen. "In thee shall all families of the earth be blessed" (Gen. 12:3). God was intervening in history for the reason that He wanted to bring blessing to the race that had turned away from Him. This involved blessing Abram, making his name great, and building a great nation from his descendants. All of this has come to pass. Every word spoken to the patriarch is worthy of respect and careful study.

As an indication of the importance of the details found in the call of Abram, history has repeatedly seen the fulfillment of the statement, "I will bless them that bless thee, and curse him that curseth thee" (Gen. 12:3). Nations that attacked or persecuted the Jewish people have perished. Assyria and Babylon are examples from ancient times. The decline of Spain is usually dated from the year 1492, when all Jews were expelled from that country. In that year a new world was discovered, where the greatest civilization known to man was to develop in a land in which Jewish people were made welcome and allowed to exercise their gifts. Ancient and modern history is replete with examples of the blessing of God resting on nations that blessed the Jew, and the judgment of God coming on nations that cursed him.

The call of Abram, later known as Abraham, links the people of Israel and the land of Palestine for the first time. God has been pleased to bless His people when they are in their land, and the land prospers only when it is occupied by the people to whom it was given. The land yields its riches only to the Jewish nation. To understand what God is going to do with His ancient people in the future, it is necessary to know something of their relationship to Palestine in the past. Three times they have left it. Twice they have returned. When they are once more brought back, they will never again leave the land of their fathers. Each departure and return is the subject of prophecy.

Many years after the call of Abram a new revelation was given to him: "Know of a surety that thy seed shall be a stranger in a land that is not their's, and shall serve them; and they shall afflict them four hundred years; and also that nation, whom they shall serve, will I judge: and afterward shall they come out with great substance" (Gen. 15:13-14). The prophecy was fulfilled after Abram's grandson Jacob left the land with his family and went to Egypt.

The sufferings of the Jewish people as slaves in Egypt under cruel taskmasters and their deliverance after God had inflicted plagues on the Egyptians under Pharaoh form one of the best-known stories of the Bible. What is not so well known is that all of this was a part of the divine purpose. It accomplished a number of far-reaching results.

God first sent Jacob's son Joseph to Egypt, permitting his brothers to sell the boy into slavery there so that he could rise to the position of prime minister. As he said to his brothers afterward, "God sent me before you to preserve you a posterity in the earth, and to save your lives by a great deliverance" (Gen. 45:7). Next, the Lord brought famine to Palestine, where Jacob and his family lived, which forced the patriarch to leave the land. He left with divine approval. God said to him, "Fear not to go down into Egypt; for I will there make of thee a great nation" (Gen. 46:3).

Several things may be said about this. Had the family of Jacob continued to live in the land as a minority group among the pagan nations of Canaan, they faced the danger of assimilation, which was contrary to the divine plan for them. After they became residents of Egypt, they were preserved as a separate people by their despised status as shepherds, and, later, as slaves. In the providence of God, every shepherd was an abomination to the Egyptians (Gen. 46:34). That same providence prepared the Jews for nationhood in the most advanced civilization of the day.

A little company of 70 farmers and herdsmen left Palestine. When their descendants left Egypt 400 years later they numbered perhaps 2 million persons, because there were 600,000 men in addition to the children (Exod. 12:37). They possessed flocks, herds of cattle, and sufficient wealth to enable them to build a strong new nation in the promised land. The groundwork had been laid for the long and glorious history of the Jewish people, and they had seen a demonstration of the power of their God. It made such a deep impression on them that throughout the Old Testament there are many scores of references to the Exodus and the marvelous experiences attending the beginnings of the nation.

The prophecy of the first departure from the land and the first restoration was given through Abram, the first man in the Bible to be called a Hebrew. It carried the story of the Jews forward more than five hundred years to the days of Moses, who completed its fulfillment by leading the people out of Egypt. Then, before the people of Israel had even entered their promised land, God gave to Moses the prophecy of a second departure from the land. "The LORD shall bring thee, and thy king which thou shalt set over thee, unto a nation which neither thou nor thy fathers have known; and there shalt thou serve other gods, wood and stone" (Deut. 28:36).

Some four centuries passed. David the king sat on the throne, followed by Solomon. The nation split in two, with the kingdom of Israel in the north and the kingdom of Judah in the south. As kings came and went, spiritual and moral deterioration increased. Eventually the Assyrians took captive the northern kingdom. Afterward Babylon came and carried away the people of the southern kingdom. These sad records are found in the closing chapters of 2 Kings and 2 Chronicles.

It was not given to Moses to know when these captivities would take place or how long his people would be absent from their land. When the time of fulfillment had come, a new prophet spoke for God in Israel. His name was Jeremiah, and to him was revealed the time element in the second departure. We read "The word that came to Jeremiah concerning all the people of Judah in the fourth year of Jehoiakim the son of Josiah king of Judah, that was the first year of Nebuchadrezzar king of Babylon. . . . this whole land shall be a desolation, and an astonishment; and these nations shall serve the king of Babylon seventy years" (Jer. 25:1, 11). To this was added a further word: "Thus saith the LORD, That after seventy years be accomplished at Babylon I will visit you, and perform my good word toward you, in causing you to return to this place" (Jer. 29:10).

When the announced period of time was nearly over, God began to move providentially to bring about the fulfillment of His promise. Among the captives in the land of Babylon was Daniel the prophet. Like all godly Jews, he was in the habit of reading the Scriptures. One day his attention was arrested by these verses in the scroll of Jeremiah. He recorded his experience later.

> In the first year of Darius the son of Ahasuerus, of the seed of the Medes, which was made king over the realm of the Chaldeans; in the first year of his reign I Daniel understood by books the number of the years, whereof the word of the LORD came to Jeremiah the prophet, that he would accomplish seventy years in the desolations of Jerusalem (Dan. 9:1-2).

Daniel accepted this revelation without question. As a godly Jew he knew that when God is about to do something in the earth He stirs up the hearts of His people to pray that it may come to pass. Daniel, and doubtless many other believing Jews in Babylon who knew of the prophecy, immediately began to seek the face of the Lord in earnest, believing prayer. The words he uttered, recorded in the ninth chapter, form a document often studied by Jews and Christians.

At the same time that God began to stir the hearts of His own people to pray for deliverance, He also began to work in the heart of Cyrus, king of Persia.

> Now in the first year of Cyrus king of Persia, that the
> word of the LORD by the mouth of Jeremiah might
> be fulfilled, the LORD stirred up the spirit of Cyrus
> king of Persia, that he made a proclamation
> throughout all his kingdom, and put it also in writ-
> ing, saying, Thus saith Cyrus king of Persia, The
> LORD God of heaven hath given me all the king-
> doms of the earth; and he hath charged me to
> build him an house at Jerusalem, which is in
> Judah. Who is there among you of all his people?
> his God be with him, and let him go up to
> Jerusalem, which is in Judah, and build the house
> of the LORD God of Israel (he is the God,) which is in
> Jerusalem (Ezra 1:1-3).

The proclamation of Cyrus created a great stir
among the Jews. More than forty thousand of them
left the land of their captivity. They returned to
Jerusalem to build the altar of the Lord and, eventually, the temple. Some years afterward, during the
reign of Artaxerxes, Ezra went to Jerusalem carrying
silver and gold provided by the Persian king.
Nehemiah, cupbearer to the king, was also encouraged to go to Palestine and rebuild the walls and the
city of Jerusalem. The descendants of those Jews
who returned from captivity occupied the land of
Palestine for the next five hundred years under the
rulership of Persia, Greece, Syria, Egypt, and Rome.
They were present in the land when the events described in the New Testament took place. In A.D. 70
the Roman legions under Titus destroyed Jerusalem, killed many of the inhabitants of the Holy
Land, and scattered the rest all over the empire as
captives and slaves, a dispersion that continues today.

This third and last departure by the Jews from

their promised land, along with their final restoration, is the theme of a great many prophecies. It first appeared in the words of Moses: "The LORD shall scatter thee among all people, from the one end of the earth even unto the other. . . . the LORD thy God will turn thy captivity, and have compassion upon thee, and will return and gather thee from all the nations. . . . And the LORD thy God will bring thee into the land which thy fathers possessed, and thou shalt possess it" (Deut. 28:64; 30:3, 5).

One notable thing about this vast body of prophecy is that it never included a time element. Moses was told the first departure was to be for 400 years. It was revealed to Jeremiah that the second departure would last 70 years. No prophet tells us how long the present dispersion is to continue. Indefinite expressions take the place of exact figures. When Hosea spoke of it he said, "For the children of Israel shall abide many days without a king, and without a prince, and without a sacrifice, and without an image, and without an ephod, and without teraphim: afterward shall the children of Israel return, and seek the LORD their God, and David their king; and shall fear the LORD and his goodness in the latter days" (Hos. 3:4-5).

Some think there may be a hidden reference to the approximate length of these "many days" in another passage in Hosea: "After two days will he revive us: in the third day he will raise us up, and we shall live in his sight" (Hos. 6:2). It has been suggested that because "one day is with the Lord as a thousand years, and a thousand years as one day," (2 Pet. 3:8; see also Ps. 90:4), the two days of Hosea may represent 2,000 years, and his third day may refer to 1,000 years of life in the presence of the Lord during His Kingdom, popularly called the Millennium, which is Latin for "a thousand years."

Such an obscure passage, of course, does not provide any basis for calculating the time of the divine regathering of Israel or the return of the Lord that is to precede it. The New Testament continues the intentional silence of the Old. In a context dealing with "the coming of the Son of man" and His gathering together of His elect, the statement is found, "of that day and hour knoweth no man, no, not the angels of heaven, but my Father only" (Matt. 24:36).

Some of the scores of paragraphs in the Bible that speak of the future regathering of Israel and their restoration to the land are very well known. "He that scattered Israel will gather him" (Jer. 31:10). "I will take you from among the heathen, and gather you out of all countries, and will bring you into your own land" (Ezek. 36:24). "I will cause them to return to the land that I gave to their fathers, and they shall possess it" (Jer. 30:3*b*).

The New Testament is just as clear and specific. Forty years before the fall of Jerusalem the Lord said, "They . . . shall be led away captive into all nations" (Luke 21:24). Again, "He shall send his angels with a great sound of a trumpet, and they shall gather together his elect from the four winds, from one end of heaven to the other" (Matt. 24:31). It is noteworthy that the Lord here used the language of Old Testament prophecy (Deut. 30:4; Ezek. 5:10; 37:9).

So much has been revealed concerning the events accompanying the regathering and restoration that it is necessary to examine the record in some detail, beginning with a look at the people of Israel during the present age. Scripture gives an extended explanation for the setting aside of Israel as a nation during the present age of the church, and there is a certain amount of truth revealed that has a definite bearing on the condition of the Jews during their long dispersion.

4

The Present Age

The Old Testament contains no prophecies of the present age as such, which began on the day of Pentecost when the Holy Spirit descended from heaven at Jerusalem to dwell in His church. The prophets spoke of the removal of the people of Israel from their land (Jer. 24:9), of an extended gap in their history when the ancient sacrifices would no more be offered (Hos. 3:4), of the desolation of their land, and of a divinely imposed blindness (Isa. 6:9-12; John 12:38-41). There are references to a coming time of blessing for the Gentiles, of tribulation in the latter days, and of the coming of Messiah to establish His kingdom. We look in vain for any light on what God would be doing while the Jewish people were set aside. The church is not mentioned even once in the Old Testament.

What God does today is "according to the revelation of the mystery, which was kept secret since the world began, but now is made manifest" (Rom. 16:25-26). The word *mystery* is a New Testament term with a special meaning. It is not something mysterious but rather something not previously made known to the human race and unattainable by human reason. God's purpose today "in other ages was not made known unto the sons of men, as it is now revealed unto his holy apostles and prophets by the Spirit; that the Gentiles should be fellowheirs, and of the same body, and partakers of his promise in Christ by the gospel" (Eph. 3:5-6).

God has not changed, nor has He altered His revealed purposes for the Jews. They were His chosen people in ancient times, and "the LORD will have mercy on Jacob, and will yet choose Israel, and set them in their own land" (Isa. 14:1). He "shall choose Jerusalem again" (Zech. 2:12). For a season, He is pleased to make no difference between Jew and Gentile (Rom. 10:12). He is choosing individuals from among all mankind on the basis of their acceptance of the gospel, which is the good news that He gave His Son to die for our sins in accordance with the Scriptures. God has set before those individuals a destiny that is altogether different from the destiny awaiting godly Israelites.

God has introduced a new age, and no explanation of what has happened to the Jewish people during the centuries of their scattering can account for the wonderful fact except the explanation found in the Bible. The present age, unannounced by the prophets of Israel, must be completed before God resumes His activities on behalf of His ancient people. In the light of the revelation given in the New Testament, it is a remarkable fact, never guessed by the prophets, that the language of prophecy was phrased in such a way as to allow for an intercalation; that is, a period of time during which Israel would no longer be in the center of the stage.

The apostle Peter commented on this fact when he said the prophets inquired and searched diligently into the meaning of what they had written about "the sufferings of Christ, and the glory that should follow" (1 Pet. 1:10-11). They did not perceive that Messiah must suffer before entering into His glory, or that many hundreds of years were to elapse before His glorious kingdom would be established. Some Jewish scholars who were aware of this double line of truth about the Messiah attempted to solve the problem by assuming there would be two Messiahs, one who would suffer and one who would reign.

When we examine the language used by Moses as he wrote of Israel's scattering and ultimate regathering, we discover that his words provide for a gap in time of unknown length between the predicted blessing and curse and the return of the Lord to gather together His scattered people (Deut. 30:1-3). After Daniel wrote about the destruction of Jerusalem following the "cutting off" of Messiah, he immediately began to describe events that are to take place during the closing seven years of Israel's history, such as the setting up of the abomination of desolation. There is a distinct break in the text between these two verses that allows for the introduction of the present age before the final years begin (Dan. 9:26-27).

Perhaps the best-known of such passages is Isaiah's Messianic prophecy in which he spoke of "the acceptable year of the LORD, and the day of vengeance of our God" (Isa. 61:1-2; see also Luke

4:16-21). Jesus began his ministry in Nazareth by reading this part of Isaiah, but He stopped reading at the comma between the two phrases. The reason was that He had come to proclaim "the acceptable year of the Lord," during which God was going to accept all who came to Him, Gentiles as well as Jews. He had not come to proclaim the day of vengeance. That must await the latter days and His return to the earth, as even Moses taught (Deut. 30:7). The fact that He stopped reading where He did is an illustration of the importance of noticing the exact words, and even the punctuation, of prophecy. It is also a good example of the way in which prophecy was written to permit the unsuspected introduction of a new age and a new purpose, here indicated only by the comma in the English text.

Although the Old Testament did not announce the coming of the present age in God's unfolding program, a number of statements were made revealing something of Israel's situation during the centuries when they were destined to be wanderers on the face of the earth. There is a whole body of passages declaring God's purpose to preserve His people during the time they are set aside. He said, "I will preserve thee" (Isa. 49:8), "I will not utterly destroy the house of Jacob" (Amos 9:8). This is in spite of the fact that when they were removed to all the kingdoms of the earth, they were to become "a curse, and an astonishment, and an hissing, and a reproach, among all the nations whither I have driven them" (Jer. 29:18). No matter how strong anti-Semitism may become, or how powerful the forces seeking to destroy the Jews, they are to continue as a people distinct from all others. God said about the movement of the sun, moon, and stars, "If those ordinances depart from before me, saith the LORD, then the seed of Israel also shall cease from being a nation before me for ever" (Jer. 31:36).

It could be anticipated that Jewish people would be known for their ability to gain wealth during the present age because God has never withdrawn the power He gave them to do this at the beginning of their history. It could also be expected that they would continue to observe their own customs and religious rites over the centuries. God said through Moses, "Ye shall observe the feast of unleavened bread . . . in your generations by an ordinance for ever" (Exod. 12:17). They eat kosher foods in an effort to respect the strict dietary laws of their ancestors. Their wisdom is a foregone conclusion; God gave it to them, and the nations have always recognized it (Deut. 4:6; Prov. 2:6).

Moses' sorrowful words about the general condition of the people of Israel during their long dispersion have often been fulfilled.

> Among these nations shalt thou find no ease, neither shall the sole of thy foot have rest: but the LORD shall give thee there a trembling heart, and failing of eyes, and sorrow of mind: and thy life shall hang in doubt before thee; and thou shalt fear day and night, and shalt have none assurance of thy life: in the morning thou shalt say, Would God it were even! and at even thou shalt say, Would God it were morning! (Deut. 28:65-67).

Jeremiah's prophecy also frequently has been an accurate description of scattered Israel. God said, "I will deliver them to be removed into all the king-

doms of the earth for their hurt, to be a reproach
and a proverb, a taunt and a curse, in all places
whither I shall drive them" (Jer. 24:9). Nevertheless,
another word of the Lord also has been shown to be
true: "No weapon that is formed against thee shall
prosper" (Isa. 54:17).

Some of the Psalms are particularly suited to the
Jewish people today. They use them in their worship
services. Their sorrowful and bitter cry is expressed
again and again. Why has God turned away from
them (Pss. 10:1; 44:11; 74:1, 11)? Why is His hand
withdrawn? Why are they scattered among the nations? Puzzled as they are over their apparent aban-
donment by God, Isaiah offers the assurance that
this is only temporary. He quoted the Lord's words:
"For a small moment have I forsaken thee; but with
great mercies will I gather thee. In a little wrath I hid
my face from thee for a moment; but with everlasting kindness will I have mercy on thee" (Isa. 54:7-8).
The contrast between terms is striking. The "moment" during which the Lord has forsaken His ancient people is small; the mercies He will show when
Israel is regathered are great. God's wrath is described as little, but His kindness when He shows
mercy is to be everlasting.

An entire chapter in the New Testament is given
to explain why "God hath not cast away his people
which he foreknew" (Rom. 11:2, 15-24). He has
turned away His face from them for a predeter-
mined time, but they have not been abandoned. As
with the branches of an olive tree, they have been
broken off, and believing Gentiles have been
"grafted in" to partake of God's favor. There is a
believing remnant of Jews today, and the nation is

going to be grafted in again someday. We are living in the age when salvation has been brought to the Gentiles because of the fall of the Jews from their place of blessing. The apostle Paul raises the question: If the temporary rejection of the Jews has meant the reconciling of the world, what will their restoration mean? Hundreds of pages of Scripture are devoted to the answer to this question.

An interesting statement about the Jewish people during the present time appears in Romans 11:25: "Blindness in part is happened to Israel, until the fulness of the Gentiles be come in." It is regarded as a comment on the judgment announced in Isaiah 6:10, "Make the heart of this people fat, and make their ears heavy, and shut their eyes; lest they see with their eyes, and hear with their ears, and understand with their heart, and convert, and be healed." "Blindness" is translated "a partial hardening" in some of the more recent translations. The term in the original evidently refers to a hardening of some Jews rather than a partial hardening, or blindness, of all. It is God who gives eyes to see and ears to hear. Whatever this "blindness in part" may be, it will be lifted someday, when the fullness of the Gentiles is come in. "The fullness of the Gentiles" is commonly understood to refer to the completion of God's present purpose to take out of Gentile nations a people for His name.

As the age draws to a close, we may look for a number of indications that this is so. What is written about the people of Israel during the period of tribulation to follow the present age will manifest its beginnings before that period starts. For example, Palestine will be populated by Jews during the Tribulation, and Jerusalem will belong to them. It takes time for such things to happen. Since they have happened in our own generation, we seem to be living in the time of the end. The land is to become fruitful when it is cultivated by its ancient owners. Prosperity is to be such as will excite the envy of other nations. The land and its people will become very important to all the nations of the earth.

5

Modern Israel

For eighteen centuries, from A.D. 70 to about 1850, it seemed impossible that the scattered people of Israel could ever become a nation again. In the nineteenth century, nationalism became a mighty force in the world. More than ever, the Jews were not allowed to feel at home in the nations in which they lived. They were regarded as intruders in many countries. They also began to see that their spiritual heritage was endangered by the pressure of the non-Jewish environment.

Altogether apart from such influences, in the mid-nineteenth century something began to happen to the Jewish people, particularly in Europe. There came a growing conviction that the time was approaching when they would be returning to Palestine. A number of publications appeared advocating such a return. Two books issued in 1862 exercised a strong influence, (*Rome and Jerusalem*, by Moses Hess, and *The Loving Quest for Zion*, by Hirsch Kalischer), and ten thousand Jews were settled in the Holy Land. A colony was founded in 1869 called Mikveh Yisrael, "The Hope of Israel." A monthly magazine called *Har-Shahar*, "*The Dawn*," was founded, proclaiming that assimilation was a failure, equality of Jews and Gentiles was a mirage, and nationhood was desirable; after the pogroms in Russia in 1881-82, the magazine said nationhood was essential.

Christians helped to stimulate this movement. Many of them believed a return of the Jews to Palestine would be a step toward the realization of the Messianic hope. In England, a popular novel dealing with the rebirth of the Jewish nation made a deep impression (*Daniel Deronda*, by George Eliot). One reason the book was so well received was that the Turkish Empire had begun to crumble, and England wanted to see Palestine populated by friendly Jews.

Prominent Jewish leaders stirred up the people. Because of anti-Semitism, Leo Pinkster, a Russian Jewish physician, electrified his people with a call to declare themselves a nation, secure their homeland, and gain recognition by other nations. Baron Rothschild became a founder of Jewish colonies in Palestine, beginning in 1878. A revival of Jewish culture and the Hebrew language took place. Lord Shaftesbury said in a famous appeal to Queen Victoria, "There is a country without a nation, and God now . . . directs us to a nation without a country. . . . The world can be redeemed only by the redemption of Israel, and Israel can only be redeemed by reunion with its land." For the first time since the days of Cyrus, a great government had hailed the Jews as one of the family of nations.

The noted newspaper writer Theodor Herzl was astonished and puzzled by anti-Semitism in France at the time of the Dreyfus trial. He wrote a pamphlet that created a sensation, "Der Judenstaat," meaning "The Jewish State." In it he argued that since the Jews were a nation, they ought to organize and secure a homeland, preferably Palestine. He called for a congress to meet in Basel, Switzerland, on August 29, 1897. There the Zionist movement was born. Its aim: "Zionism seeks to establish for the Jewish people a publicly recognized, legally secured home in Palestine." Branches of the movement were formed in most nations. An annual congress was held thereafter amid great enthusiasm.

It has been claimed with some reason that Zionism, humanly speaking, owed its origin largely to the efforts of a Christian student of prophecy and lover of Israel. William E. Blackstone, author of the widely popular work *Jesus is Coming*, presented to President Harrison on March 5, 1891, a memorial urging that he use his good offices with the governments of Europe to arrange an international conference regarding the establishing of a national home for the Jews in Palestine. The memorial was signed by many American notables, and representatives of nearly the entire American press. The signees of the memorial may rightly be called precursors of Theodor Herzl.

In 1885 a leading Jewish lawyer from Bessarabia, Joseph Rabinowitz, vacationed in Palestine. Someone had given him a New Testament as a guidebook. As he sat on the Mount of Olives, pondering the scattering and persecution of his people and reading the Testament, it suddenly dawned on him that Jesus of Nazareth was the true Messiah of Israel. He returned to Russia a Christian, moving great audiences by his public testimony to the saving power of the Lord as the One who had fulfilled Old Testament prophecy concerning the Messiah. He was invited to speak at Bible conferences in other countries, and became a widely sought preacher in America. Franz Delitzsch, the great Bible expositor and outstanding Jewish scholar whose commentaries are still studied, said of Rabinowitz that he was "the first ripe fig on the long barren tree of Israel, a sign that summer is nigh. Rabinowitz is a star in the firmament of his people."

There were other notable conversions among the Jews at that same time. The great Jewish expositors arose during this period: Delitzsch, Baron, Edersheim, Saphir, Neander. By the year 1900, Christian magazines reported that 250 churches in England and 125 in America were pastored by Jewish Christians. Modern missions to the Jews developed, first in Europe, then in America, and later around the world. The doctrine of the Lord's return was rediscovered late in the nineteenth century after having been lost for centuries. Bible conferences on prophecy began and were attended by great crowds. A literature was developed that sought to cast light on the neglected prophecies of the Bible.

By 1914 some eighty thousand Jews had returned to Palestine. In 1917 the British took Palestine from Turkey. On November 2, 1917 the Balfour Declaration was issued. "His Majesty's government views with favor the establishment in Palestine of a national home for the Jewish people, and will use their best endeavours to facilitate the establishing of the object."

During the First World War a Russian Jew, Chaim Weizmann, discovered a method for producing acetone, an ingredient of TNT, from maize. He gave his discovery to the British government in return for its promise to use its power and influence to secure a homeland for the Jews in their ancient land. In 1925 the flag of Israel floated over the ocean for the first time. In 1927 the first Jewish money was coined. In 1929 electricity was brought into the city of Jerusalem. In 1922 Eliezer ben Yehudah died, after working forty years to restore Hebrew as the national language. When he died, a census showed that 96 percent of the Jews then in the land claimed Hebrew as their mother tongue.

On November 2, 1947 the United Nations accepted the principle of establishing a Jewish state in Palestine. On May 14, 1948 the State of Israel was called into being in Tel Aviv after efforts to implement the decision of the United Nations had failed. Chaim Weizmann was made the first president. David Ben Gurion became a world figure as Israel's greatest statesman. When the nation was born, Israel was attacked by the armies of Egypt, Iraq, Syria, Lebanon, Jordan, and Saudi Arabia. The victory of the Jewish forces astounded the world, as did the prosperity of the new nation.

This summary of a few facts about modern Israel is given to underline the fact that wonderful things have been happening to the Jews after many centuries of obscurity and weakness. Jews and Christians all over the world are convinced that this concentration of unusual events indicates a change of great importance to Israel's future has been taking place. When these happenings are viewed in the light of the picture drawn in the Bible of Israel's latter days, their significance cannot be denied.

6

The Latter Days

The world is strewn with the wreckage of past civilizations. Just as uncounted ancient nations have grown old and died, some of those existing in this atomic age will also pass away. The Bible tells us how it is going to happen. Prophecies both extensive and detailed have been written about the end of 6,000 years of recorded history, and perhaps many more. God has been pleased to speak at length concerning the death throes of the world we have known. The revealed facts are far different from popular notions about "the end of the world." Some imagine an atomic holocaust will wipe out the human race. Others suppose it will end with a whimper instead of a bang. The Bible says God will ultimately destroy the world by fire (2 Pet. 3:10-12; see also Isa. 65:17), but not until there have been 1,000 years of peace on earth after the Lord has returned.

God's purpose in the present age is to take out from mankind "a people for his name" (Acts 15:14). No one knows how long this is going to

take, and there are no clues in Scripture. Not even
the angels know the day or the hour when the
events will begin that are to follow the completion of
the present stage of God's plan. He is forming a new
company of redeemed people distinct from the
people of Israel and the Gentiles who will continue
to populate the earth as long as it stands.

When God has finally chosen the last member of
the elect group called the church, He will resume
His dealings with Israel and the nations.

> And to this agree the words of the prophets; as it is
> written, after this I will return, and will build again
> the tabernacle of David, which is fallen down; and I
> will build again the ruins thereof, and I will set it up:
> that the residue of men might seek after the Lord,
> and all the Gentiles, upon whom my name is called,
> saith the Lord, who doeth all these things. Known
> unto God are all his works from the beginning of
> the world (Acts 15:15-18; see also Amos 9:11-12).

If we had only this text, we might assume the
return of the Lord will follow immediately after the
end of the church age, when all believers, living and
dead, are translated from the earth to meet the Lord
in the air as He descends from heaven to meet
them. Other Scriptures, however, make it clear that
this will not be the case. An extended series of
events is to intervene between the completion of
God's purpose for this present age and the beginning of the execution of His purposes for the age to
come. The Bible speaks of the last days of the
church and the last days of Israel. The characteristics of the two periods are in striking contrast to
each other.

The last days of the church will have come when

the great apostasy exists, false teachers have large followings, a world religious organization has formed, perilous times have come, the return of the Lord is scoffed at, and the gospel has reached every people and nation.

When conditions such as these prevail, at some unknown moment the Lord is going to descend from heaven to the air. He will call believers away from earth to meet Him and be with Him forever (1 Thess. 4:13-18). In a moment so brief it is likened to the twinkling of an eye, each of His people is to receive a new, resurrection body, described in some detail in the New Testament (1 Cor. 15:35-53). Although some think the whole world will hear the sounds of the trump of God, the voice of the archangel, and the shout of the Lord that initiate this translation of believers, others expect the age to end as quietly as it began, without benefit of prophecy and without fanfare.

The nature of the church is widely misunderstood. It is a divinely chosen company of people that has been growing invisibly for nearly two thousand years, as God has selected one individual after another from the human race. Parallel to this growth of an elect body of believers, a human organization has appeared, known to the world as the church, a visible, ecclesiastical organization. Christianity ought not to be judged by what this organization, or any part of it, may have said or done. When the true church of God is gone from the earth, the ecclesiastical church will remain behind. It will have turned away from revealed truth. Its existence will finally be terminated by divine judgment.

With the introduction of the church to the pages

of Scripture, the human race was divided into three parts: the Jew, the Gentile, and the church of God (1 Cor. 10:32). Each of these is to pass through its last days, as described in the Bible. After the age of the church has ended with the coming of the Lord in the air to remove all believers from the earth, the Jews will occupy the center of the stage as God begins to prepare them for the coming of the kingdom. A complex series of events will begin to unfold.

Old Testament prophecy mentions the last, or latter, days of Israel at least fifteen times. No information is given by which anyone can say when those days will come, although the event that ushers them in is briefly described. Seven years out of Israel's last days are set apart for particular mention, so filled with strange and wonderful happenings that whole volumes have been written about them. For example, a powerful dictator will emerge who will attack the people of Israel in their land, persecute them all over the world, and then be crushed by divine intervention before the Lord establishes His own kingdom.

General signs of the approach of the last days include tendencies toward international cooperation such as is now seen in the United Nations, the breakdown of barriers among European countries (perhaps illustrated by the Common Market), the awakening of the peoples of Asia and Africa, and the emergence of Russia as a powerful and warlike force in the north. There are to be movements toward a world economy and a world religion. Distress and perplexity of nations is to follow the bankruptcy of world leadership. Knowledge will increase, and

travel will be commonplace. War, famine, earthquake, and pestilence are to become increasingly
severe as the end approaches.

Some students have assumed the events of the
last days are to begin immediately following the
translation of the church to meet the Lord. That is
doubtless possible, but the calling away of the
church is not said to be a sign by which other events
can be dated. There is no clear statement about
whether or not prophecies concerning the last days
of Israel begin to unfold at that time. The mills of
God grind slowly. He may interpose an interval of
unknown length between the end of the age of the
church and the first of the events predicted for the
latter days. In any case, the fulfillment of God's purposes for Israel must await the completion of His
purpose for the present age.

The last days are set apart in Scripture from other
periods. More space is given to them than to any
other comparable segment of history, except for the
gospel record of the life and times of Jesus of
Nazareth. They form a part of the "day of the Lord,"
that extended period during which the Lord fulfills
every prophecy having to do with the preparation for
the kingdom and its establishment in the earth.

The earliest mention of the latter days is found in
the books of Moses. Balaam prophesied that a Star
and Scepter will rise out of Israel at that time, He
who shall have dominion (Num. 24:14-19). Tribulation will come upon the Jews; evil is to befall them.
Job knew his Redeemer would stand upon the earth
in the latter days (Job 19:25). Daniel explained to
Nebuchadnezzar what shall be in those days (Dan.
2:28), and to Daniel came an angel with the an-

nouncement, "I am come to make thee understand what shall befall thy people in the latter days" (Dan. 10:14). Isaiah and Micah both wrote about the Lord's house being established in Jerusalem at that time, and the law going forth out of Zion (Isa. 2:1-4; Mic. 4:1-5). To such passages as these, where the last days are specifically mentioned, must be added vast sections of the prophetic Word describing particular events destined to take place at that time.

It is a solemnizing revelation that the evil that is to befall the Jewish people in the end times is to be far worse than anything they have known throughout centuries of devilish persecution. As we read about that dreadful period of history in Scripture, intellectual curiosity must not be permitted to make us forget this fact. Daniel wrote, "there shall be a time of trouble, such as never was since there was a nation even to that same time: and at that time thy people shall be delivered" (Dan. 12:1). This promise of help from the God of Israel is often repeated. As Moses wrote,

> When thou art in tribulation, and all these things are come upon thee, even in the latter days, if thou turn to the LORD thy God, and shalt be obedient unto his voice; (For the LORD thy God is a merciful God;) he will not forsake thee, neither destroy thee, nor forget the covenant of thy fathers which he sware unto them (Deut. 4:30-31).

As we examine briefly some of what is written about this coming time of crisis and fulfillment in the long history of God's ancient people, we shall learn that it is to be concentrated within a specific and limited period. God has been pleased to reveal how it will begin, what it will be like, and when and

how it will end. The conclusion of Israel's time of
tribulation marks the beginning of the blessings
about which her people have sung for centuries.
The manifestation of Israel's Messiah in His glory
will be the outstanding climactic event in all human
history, as the prophets long ago foretold.

7

The Seventieth Week of Daniel

A coming period of seven years in the experience of the Jews is set apart from all others in Scripture and mentioned with such frequency that it must be of great importance in the divine program. It often appears in the Old Testament prophets, and it is referred to in some way by every New Testament writer. Christ emphasized it in His Olivet discourse. The book of Revelation is largely a description of its leading events and personages.

These final seven years conclude the history of the human race prior to the setting up of Messiah's Kingdom. They introduce that extended period called "the day of the Lord," a phrase found in twelve books of the Bible. Various descriptive terms are used by the prophets when they speak of it. It is the pouring out of destruction from the Almighty (Joel 1:15), when "the LORD cometh out of his place to punish the inhabitants of the earth for their iniquity" (Isa. 26:21). It is "the time of Jacob's trouble" (Jer. 30:7), a period of unparalleled distress for the nations (Luke 21:25). The whole earth will be terribly shaken at that time (Isa. 2:19). Vast multitudes will perish before this great day of the wrath of the Lamb has run its course.

All nature is drawn upon to describe those dark days. We read of smoke, fire, brimstone, great hail, lightning, darkness, and evil beasts. Stars will fall from above, the earth will shake beneath, and the greatest earthquake in history will take place. Man's efforts to govern himself will come to an end, with sights never before seen on land or sea. The throne of God will dominate the scene. Voices and trumpet blasts will come from heaven. Plagues will be visited on the human race. The supernatural will burst in on the earth. Angels and demons will become active. The bottomless pit will be opened. Frightful signs will become visible to men. Fearful announcements will be made from the sky.

Trouble will be sent on all the world, to try those who dwell on the earth. God will punish the world for its iniquity. Peace will be taken from among men. An angel will cry, "Woe, woe, woe, to the inhabiters of the earth" (Rev. 8:13). Men hide in holes of the rocks and dens of the mountains (Rev. 6:15). The devil and his angels will be cast into the earth (Rev. 12:9). Infernal locusts will come out of the smoke of the pit to bring torment (Rev. 9:1-6).

The first reference in the Bible to a specific time of tribulation was written by Moses. He related it to Israel and placed it in the latter days (Deut. 4:30). The last use of the expression is found in the book of Revelation, with reference to a great multitude who come out of the Great Tribulation, "of all nations, and kindreds, and people, and tongues" (Rev. 7:9-14).

Much has been written on why students of the Scriptures speak of the closing period of Israel's prophetic history as seven years in length. The figure is taken from Daniel 9:24-27, the most important chronological passage in all Bible prophecy. It was revealed to Daniel that everlasting righteousness would finally come to the Jews at the conclusion of a historical period totaling seventy weeks, or sevens of years, beginning with a specific event whose occurrence happens to be one of the best-confirmed dates in history. That event was the issuing of a command by Artaxerxes to restore and to build Jerusalem in 445 B.C.

After sixty-nine of these "weeks," totaling 483 years, Messiah was to be cut off, and afterward Jerusalem was to be destroyed (Dan. 9:25-26). These two tremendous events occurred when Jesus of Nazareth was crucified in approximately A.D. 30, and when the city fell to Titus forty years later. The exactitude of Daniel's prediction has amazed students for centuries. A careful study of the chronology is found in *The Coming Prince*, by Sir Robert Anderson. It is apparent that the 483 years ended at some time during the days when Jesus walked the earth.

The seventieth week, separated in the text from the previous sixty-nine weeks (Dan. 9:27), is awaiting fulfillment in the latter days, following the conclusion of the present age, during which Israel is set aside and God is carrying out a new purpose by calling out the church from all mankind. At that time, "the prince that shall come" (Dan. 9:26) will enter into a covenant, or treaty, with "many" Jews, break his covenant after three and one-half years have passed, put a stop to Jewish sacrifices, and set up the abomination of desolation.

The book of Revelation confirms the latter-day chronology of Daniel by describing a number of events that take place. or begin to take place, in connection with a period of 3-1/2 years. In Revelation the 3-1/2 years end with the coming of the Lord. The text refers to the 3-1/2 years as 42 months, 1,260 days, "a time, and times, and half a time" (Rev. 11:2-3; 12:6,14; 13:5). The prophetic year of the Bible is 360 days. Some scholars have advanced the theory that cataclysmic changes in our solar system took place in ancient times, changing the year of 360 days to the present 365.

The expression "the seventieth week of Daniel" has come into common use to designate the seven-year period prior to the return of the Lord, when the history of Israel will draw to a close. It will begin with the making of a "firm covenant" between a prince who shall come and many of the people of Israel. The coming prince is identified as the coming evil dictator who is to hold the whole world in thrall (2 Thess. 2:3-4). In the New Testament he is called the beast (Rev. 13:1-10) and the antichrist (1 John 2:18). The many Jews who sign the treaty are regarded as those who return to the land before the Lord returns and gathers His people to restore them to Palestine. The signing of the covenant, or treaty, implies the existence of a population in the land large enough to have formed a nation.

It is wonderful to be living in the generation that has witnessed the establishment of a Hebrew nation in the land for the first time in nearly twenty-five hundred years, independent of Gentile control. It is most interesting to notice that no prophecy announces the return of such a company of Jews to Palestine as has returned during the twentieth century, and yet prophecy does indicate the presence of such a population in the last days. The prophesied divine regathering will not take place until after the return of the Lord. A large body of Scripture is devoted to it. The presence in the land of a Jewish nation at the time of the coming of the Lord is made the subject of a smaller revelation.

When Ezekiel wrote about an invasion of Palestine in the latter days he mentioned that God will call the people of the land "my people of Israel" (Ezek. 38:16). They will have gathered out of the nations, but not as the result of direct divine intervention. Not until some time after the invasion will the regathering about which Moses spoke take place (Ezek. 39:25-29). We are not told why or how these people will come to Palestine, but they apparently will be there in a state of unbelief. They will be numerous and prosperous enough to be invaded by large armies.

Joel wrote about a time when the day of the Lord will be at hand. The inhabitants of Palestine will be called "children of Zion." Again, we are not informed where they will come from. The day of the Lord will be so terrible that the Lord will call the Jews to turn to Him in prayer. The absence of divine favor is seen in the words of their enemies, "Where is their God?" Not until afterward will the Lord become active in overthrowing the northern army of invaders, blessing His people, and judging the nations (Joel 2:17-23; 3:1-2).

The prophet Zechariah wrote of "the inhabitants

of Jerusalem" at the time all nations come together against the city. These inhabitants will be Jewish. They will mourn as they look on their returning Messiah, who will come to the Mount of Olives to deliver them. It is clear that many Jews will then live in the land, but Scripture is silent on their number or the manner of their return. Before the Lord returns, they will be unbelieving (Zech. 12—14).

In another passage, the people in the land just before the return of the Lord are called "them which be in Judea" (Matt. 24:16). They will have a holy place, they will observe the Sabbath, and they will be troubled by false Christs and false prophets. When the Lord returns He will regather His elect people from the places where the Old Testament says He has driven them, that is, from the four winds and from one end of heaven to the other (Deut. 28:64; 30:4; Zech. 2:6; Matt. 24:27-31).

Daniel said the coming prince who breaks his treaty will "cause the sacrifice and the oblation to cease" (Dan. 9:27), which indicates the existence of a temple in Jerusalem and the restoration of the ancient Jewish sacrifices. Without making a particular point of it, the New Testament also speaks of a temple and a holy place (Matt. 24:15; 2 Thess. 2:4; Rev. 11:1-2). Christian students share with Jewish students the conviction that a new temple will some day rise in Jerusalem, in which the Jewish sacrificial system will be resumed.

Other general facts about conditions in Palestine in the latter days are found here and there throughout Scripture. The land will become fertile and fruitful under the hand of its Jewish inhabitants, being described "as the garden of Eden" (Joel 2:3). Prosperity will have come to the people. They will dwell safely without the walls, bars, and gates that protected their cities in ancient times (Ezek. 38:11-12). Jerusalem will be built up (Ps. 102:16).

Some of the things that take place during the seventieth week of Daniel are described with no reference to the exact time they occur, so it becomes a matter of opinion whether they are to be placed early or late in the week, or somewhere in between. This is the case with the setting apart by God of a large company of Hebrews for a special responsibility as the divine program begins to focus once more on Israel. He will choose 144,000 Jews, 12,000 from each of twelve tribes, and place some kind of divine seal on each individual by which he will be protected from his enemies (Rev. 7:1-8).

What the 144,000 will do is not actually revealed, but several facts indicate they will be God's evangelists, or missionaries. Immediately after this revelation we read of a great multitude of Gentiles saved out of the Great Tribulation (Rev. 7:9-14). God never leaves Himself without a witness. The church will be gone from the earth. Before and after the age of the church the Jews are His messengers; no other group is mentioned during the seventieth week. Christ said, "This gospel of the kingdom shall be preached in all the world for a witness unto all nations; and then shall the end come (Matt. 24:14).

During those terrible days the unbelieving world will be startled and angered by two strange beings who stand forth to bear witness to the truth of God (Rev. 11:3-12; see also Zech. 4:3, 11-14). They possess superhuman power. At their bidding the clouds will withhold their rain and water will be turned into blood. This is so much like the powers given Moses and Elijah that some have assumed those two men are going to appear on the earth again. It is, of course, definitely predicted that at some future time Elijah will be sent to Israel by the Lord "before the coming of the great and dreadful day of the Lord (Mal. 4:5-6). Christ also spoke of this. "Elias truly shall first come, and restore all things" (Matt. 17:11).

The judicial blindness of Israel prophesied by Isaiah and mentioned in the New Testament is to be lifted when "the fulness of the Gentiles" has come in (Rom. 11:25; see also Isa. 6:9-13). "The fulness of the Gentiles" is usually understood to mean the completion of God's present purpose to call Gentiles as members of His church. If this is so, the taking away of Israel's partial blindness will follow the end of the church age and precede the seventieth week of Daniel. The spiritual blindness resting on the entire human race will continue. Its source is at least partly satanic (2 Cor. 4:3-4); it is removed only by the Holy Spirit in the moment of individual salvation.

One other event that will take place in the last days, and evidently during the seventieth week, is the invasion of Palestine by armies from the north, as described by Ezekiel (Ezek. 38-39). This prophecy has the land primarily in view, rather than the people, and will be examined in our study of the land, but it requires mention here. It is not possible to pinpoint the time when it will take place, but one fact about it indicates that it belongs among the events we have been considering. When God intervenes to drive the invading forces out of the country,

"the house of Israel shall know that I am the LORD
their God from that day and forward (Ezek. 39:22).
This important statement links the invasion with
Moses' prophecy that the people of Israel would
recall the days of ancient times, return to the Lord,
and obey His voice according to what He commanded Moses. The tremendous impact of what
the Lord does to deliver His land and His people in
the latter days will turn the hearts of many back to
Him from within unbelieving Israel, still dispersed
among the nations at that time. Passages like
Matthew 24:10-12 indicate the presence of many
Jews who continue in a state of rebellion.

8

The Great Tribulation

The darkest period in the entire history of the world is to be the second half of the seventieth week of Daniel, who wrote, "There shall be a time of trouble, such as never was since there was a nation even to that same time" (Dan. 12:1). After quoting a phrase from Daniel and warning of its importance, the Lord said, "Then shall be great tribulation, such as was not since the beginning of the world to this time, no, nor ever shall be" (Matt. 24:21).

Several passages of Scripture emphasize the fact that the expression "the Great Tribulation" is properly applied only to the last half of the period described by Daniel, and not to the entire seven years that begin with the signing of a covenant with the prince who is to come. A climactic, supernatural event will introduce the final three and one-half years. The book of Revelation describes a war in heaven. Michael and his angels will fight against Satan and his angels. Satan will be defeated and cast out into the earth with all his evil host (Rev. 12:7-10), an event predicted in Isaiah 24:21. His role as "the accuser of our brethren" in God's presence, permitted ever since Job's day and before, will be ended (Job 1:9-11; 2:3-5).

The warning is now given, "Woe to the inhabiters of the earth and of the sea! for the devil is come down unto you, having great wrath, because he knoweth that he hath but a short time" (Rev. 12:12). The first evidence of his wrath that we are told about is a satanic persecution of Jewish people, members of the nation that gave the Messiah, who is destined to destroy the devil, to the world.

To escape such fearful persecution, these Jews will flee into the wilderness, where God will have prepared a place of refuge for them, and where He will nourish and protect them for 1,260 days, the 3-1/2 years of the Great Tribulation (Matt. 24:15-21; Rev. 12:12-17). Bible students have sometimes sought to identify this place. Their most interesting and plausible guess is that it is Petra, which is the Old Testament Sela. Carved out of steep, rocky cliffs in a hidden valley at the end of a long, narrow defile, it is so remote that its location was forgotten for centuries.

Completely frustrated in this first attempt to destroy the people he has hated over the centuries, Satan will make war with the remnant of the seed of Israel, "which keep the commandments of God, and have the testimony of Jesus Christ" (Rev. 12:17). It seems clear from this passage and from the general context that those who flee to the wilderness will be godly Jews who live in Palestine, whereas "the remnant" will be godly Jews scattered among the nations. Other texts support this view.

At the same time Satan is cast into the earth,

other events will take place that mark the beginning
of Great Tribulation for the Hebrews and the entire
world. For example, the prince who is to come will
break his covenant with the nation Israel and cause
the sacrifice and oblation to cease. The two events
are tied together by Revelation 13:1-8, where we
read that the dragon, who is Satan, will give strange
and terrible power to the evil ruler of those days.
That power will be limited by God to only forty-two
months, corresponding again to the last 3-1/2
years of Daniel's seventieth week.

It has often been pointed out that this satanically
empowered ruler is going to be a Roman prince.
"The people of the prince that shall come" (Dan.
9:26) destroyed Jerusalem. Since these people
were Roman armies, it follows that their prince will
be a Roman, coming from Italy or some other part
of the old Roman Empire. Some think he, or his
"false prophet," will be a Jew. This is based largely
on two texts. The Lord warned that during the Great
Tribulation "there shall arise false Christs, and false
prophets, and shall shew great signs and wonders;
insomuch that, if it were possible, they shall deceive
the very elect" (Matt. 24:23-26). No false messiah
could hope to be accepted by Jewish people looking for their true Messiah if he were not a Jew himself. The other passage is found in John 5:43: "I am
come in my Father's name, and ye receive me not:
if another shall come in his own name, him ye will
receive."

One notable event of the last days was chosen by
the Lord for special emphasis. He warned, "When
ye therefore shall see the abomination of desolation, spoken of by Daniel the prophet, stand in the

abomination - image of beast

holy place, (whoso readeth, let him understand:)
then let them which be in Judea flee into the mountains" (Matt. 24:15-16). This flight corresponds with
the flight occasioned by the satanic persecution
mentioned in Revelation. The placing of the abomination in the temple corresponds with the end of
the sacrifice and oblation there, after the Roman
prince breaks his covenant with the Jews.

In Old Testament days an abomination was an
image such as "the abomination of the Ammo-
nites" in 1 Kings 11:5. There is no reason for giving
it a different meaning here or for supposing it is
different from the image of the dictator of the last
days, which must be worshiped under pain of death
and which will be given both breath and speech by
satanic power (Rev. 13:14-15, NASB). When they
see the abomination, the Jewish people in the land
who honor the words of the Lord will flee, because
this is the sign He gave by which they will know that
history's worst time of tribulation is beginning.

Bible students usually place the killing of God's
two witnesses at this same time. Their supernatural
power will continue for 3-1/2 years; then they will be
killed. Their dead bodies will lie in the street of
Jerusalem for 3-1/2 days while the world looks on
and rejoices over their deaths (Rev. 11:9). There is a
surprising sidelight on this scene. As far back as the
nineteenth century, students of prophecy, because
of what is written here, anticipated the discovery of
some means whereby events occurring in the city of
Jerusalem could be viewed by people all over the
earth.

There is nothing to be gained by examining other
details concerning the sufferings of the people of

Israel in those days. The great political leader in whom they trust will turn against them, their temple worship will be brought to an end and the temple will be defiled, they will leave their homes and flee to the wilderness for safety, and there will be death in the streets.

The wrath of God will be poured out on all the earth (Rev. 16:1). The wrath of the devil will be vented on men as he realizes his time is short (Rev. 12:12). The wrath of men will be unrestrained (Gal. 5:20). In the midst of this threefold display of wrath, God will remember His ancient people. Michael, the archangel, will stand up for the Jews (Dan. 12:1). This also seems to be the time about which Isaiah's words were written, "Come, my people, enter thou into thy chambers, and shut thy doors about thee: hide thyself as it were for a little moment, until the indignation be overpast" (Isa. 26:20).

The prophet Zechariah supplied the most detailed account of how the Great Tribulation will end. As the three and one-half years draw near their conclusion, God will begin to move toward the grand consummation of what He has planned from before the foundation of the world. He will work in the hearts of the rulers of the earth so that all nations will gather against Jerusalem to battle. The city will be taken, the houses rifled, and the women ravished. Half of the population will be taken captive, half will remain (Zech. 14:1-2). The moment will finally come for God to intervene. One of the great events in time and eternity will take place.

> Then shall the Lord go forth, and fight against those nations, as when he fought in the day of battle. And his feet shall stand in that day upon the

> mount of Olives, which is before Jerusalem on the
> east, and the mount of Olives shall cleave in the
> midst thereof toward the east and toward the west,
> and there shall be a very great valley; and half of the
> mountain shall remove toward the north, and half
> of it toward the south (Zech. 14:3-4).

At last the final prophecy of Moses will be fulfilled. Many Jews will have returned to the Lord their God during the Tribulation period, and will have begun to obey His voice according to all He commanded Moses. Now He will have compassion on them and return, as He promised long ago. He will come to the earth in person; Zechariah tells us the exact spot where His feet will touch down. It is impossible to escape the parallel here with the promise made to the apostles in Acts 1:11-12. Jesus of Nazareth, who ascended to heaven from the Mount of Olives, will come in like manner as He was seen ascending, and to that same mount.

The effect of His coming will be like that of a great earthquake. The Mount of Olives will split down the middle, creating a very great valley extending eastward from Jerusalem. Through the valley the Jewish people remaining in besieged Jerusalem will make their escape, "and the LORD my God shall come, and all the saints with thee" (Zech. 14:5). It might be said that just as the nations will invade Palestine from the four quarters of the earth, to crush the Jews, so the land will be invaded from outer space by the armies of heaven to save the Jews.

As the house of David and the inhabitants of Jerusalem witness the coming of the Lord from heaven to deliver them in their hour of greatest peril,

He will pour upon them the spirit of grace and sup-
plications. They will look upon Him, and recognize
Him as the Messiah whom believing Jews and Gentiles have worshiped for centuries. In the words of
the beloved King James Version, "They shall look
upon me whom they have pierced" (Zech. 12:10).
They will mourn as one who is in bitterness for his
firstborn. "In that day there shall be a fountain
opened to the house of David and to the inhabitants
of Jerusalem for sin and for uncleanness" (Zech.
13:1).

In that day the Lord will seek to destroy all the
nations that come against Jerusalem. Zechariah
does not go into detail about their defeat. Those
details appear in Revelation 19:11-21. Heaven
opens, and One who is called The Word of God
comes forth, followed by the armies of heaven. The
name written on His garment is "KING OF KINGS,
AND LORD OF LORDS" (Rev. 19:16). The evil world
ruler will be taken, with his false prophet, and their
armies will be crushed. The Tribulation will end, Israel will be delivered, and her enemies will be destroyed. With her Messiah present in person, she will
see events rush toward their prophesied conclusion.
Several things must still take place before Messiah's
Kingdom is established.

Moses wrote that after the Lord returned He
would gather Israel from all the nations whither He
had scattered them (Deut. 30:3). This is a major
theme of prophecy, mentioned in thirteen books of
the Bible. At least twelve different words are used to
describe it. Thirty-five times we read that God will
gather the Jews. Thirty-five times it is written that He
will bring them to their own land. Twenty-three

times He turns or brings back their captivity. He will recover them, assemble them, lead them back, place them, plant them. Ezekiel, looking backward in a vision of the future, speaks of this as an accomplished fact: "I have gathered them unto their own land" (Ezek. 39:28).

Just when this regathering takes place is made perfectly clear. It will be after the Lord has returned to the earth. It will be the second time He has brought them back, the first time having been when they returned from the Babylonian captivity (Isa. 11:11). It will be after many Jews have inhabited the land in the latter days, after Palestine has been invaded by a northern confederacy and a world-shaking divine intervention has taken place. It cannot take place until after all nations have gathered against Jerusalem and taken the city. The Great Tribulation will then have run its full course. Jews all over the world will have turned to the God of their fathers, as Moses prophesied.

How the Lord is to accomplish this miracle of regathering His people is made the subject of a considerable revelation. He will do it with a mighty hand and with fury poured out, after He has searched and sought for them (Ezek. 20:34; 34:11). Some will fly as a cloud, as doves to their windows. Others will be brought by the ships of Tarshish (Isa. 60:8-9). The nations will take them and bring them (Isa. 14:2). God will gather them one by one (Isa. 27:12). He will bring them with great mercies (Isa. 54:7). They will come with weeping and supplication (Jer. 31:9). It will be the complete gathering of a great company (Jer. 31:8). God will leave none of them scattered among the Gentiles anymore (Ezek.

39:28). It will be a final, permanent restoration. They will never again be pulled out of their land (Amos 9:15).

In the light of such revelations as these, we can better understand one of the most remarkable statements in all Scripture about the divine re-gathering of the Jews. "Behold, the days come, saith the LORD, that it shall no more be said, The LORD liveth, that brought up the children of Israel . . . from the land of the north, and from all the lands whither he had driven them: and I will bring them again into their land that I gave unto their fathers" (Jer. 16:14-15). Scores of times the Old Testament refers to the miracle of the Exodus as the greatest manifestation of the power of God on behalf of His people. The final regathering after the Lord's return will surpass the wonder of the ancient Exodus in the minds of the Jewish people. The great trumpet will be blown, and angels will be sent out after the scattered tribes. Their fervent prayer will be answered, "Save us, O LORD our God, and gather us from among the heathen" (Ps. 106:47; see also Isa. 27:13 and Matt. 24:31).

It is often mistakenly assumed that the Lord will gather His people to the Holy Land, but prophecy distinguishes between the regathering and the restoration to the land. The two lines of truth were separated by Moses, and Ezekiel developed the differences. He wrote, "I will bring you out from the people, and will gather you out of the countries wherein ye are scattered. . . . And I will bring you into the wilderness of the people, and there will I plead with you face to face" (Ezek. 20:34-35).

"The wilderness of the people" is generally identified with the area in the Sinai Peninsula where the people wandered for thirty-eight years in the days of Moses. It is mentioned scores of times in the Pentateuch; no other wilderness is so frequently associated with the Jewish people. There is also a striking parallel between the scene described by Ezekiel and another that took place in ancient times, doubtless in the same wilderness.

Early in the journey from Egypt many Jews became rebellious. The Lord said of them, "Surely they shall not see the land which I sware unto their fathers, neither shall any of them that provoked me see it . . . . your carcases shall fall in this wilderness" (Num. 14:23, 29). In the similar confrontation prophesied in Ezekiel, the life of every rebellious Jew is going to end in the wilderness of the people. "I will purge out from among you the rebels, and them that transgress against me: I will bring them forth out of the country where they sojourn, and they shall not enter into the land of Israel: and ye shall know that I am the LORD, (Ezek. 20:38). To the godly Jews He says, "And ye shall know that I am the LORD, when I shall bring you into the land of Israel" (Ezek. 20:42).

A similar judgment of the people of Israel appears in the New Testament. One company called evil and unprofitable servants is cast into outer darkness where there is weeping and gnashing of teeth. A second company is made up of faithful and profitable servants. They become rulers over many things as they enter into the joy of their Lord (Matt. 24:45-51; 25:14-30). Parallel to this scene is a judgment of Gentiles, likewise divided into two groups. The unrighteous are sent into everlasting fire, whereas the righteous enter the kingdom where they enjoy life eternal (Matt. 25:31-46). The basis for this judgment of Gentiles is the way the two companies treated the brethren of Christ, believed to be Jewish people who suffered severe persecution during the Great Tribulation. A parallel passage is found in Joel 3:2.

It is clearly taught in a number of New Testament passages that before the Kingdom begins, all unrighteous persons will be cast out. The millennial reign of the Messiah will dawn without the presence of a single wicked person (Matt. 13:41-43; 47-50). Living Jews and Gentiles will enter the Kingdom together, but only those judged righteous by the Lord will enjoy that privilege.

9

Israel in the Kingdom

Men have longed for a paradise on earth ever since sin brought labor, sorrow, and death to mankind, and thorns and thistles to the ground. Their dream has been expressed in legend and song throughout the centuries. Plato described what he conceived to be a perfect city in his *Republic* in the fifth century B.C. Two thousand years later, in A.D. 1516, Sir Thomas More wrote his famous volume, *Utopia*, describing an imaginary island on which the ideal social and political state existed. The name *Utopia* was made up of two Greek words meaning "no place." It entered the language as a synonym for any state or place of ideal perfection. A hundred years later Sir Francis Bacon tried to picture an ideal commonwealth in his *New Atlantis*. Other, similar works have occasionally appeared.

While men have been dreaming and writing about a beautiful isle of nowhere, they have tended to overlook the vast revelation in the Bible about a future golden age that God has promised will

someday come to earth. It will be the glorious Kingdom over which Messiah will rule as King of kings
and Lord of lords, the Millennium expected by
Christians who know the Word, the thousand years
mentioned in the book of Revelation.

It is not generally realized how complete a picture
of the coming kingdom is found in the Scriptures
covering world government and changes in nature,
human life and its circumstances, and the unseen
world. In a book devoted to the destiny of Israel it is
not possible to develop the details of the coming
age as it relates to man and his world in general, but
something of the rich content of what is prophesied
can be indicated as a background for the place
Israel is to occupy during the Kingdom age.

Christ will rule all nations from His throne in
Jerusalem. Associated with Him in government will
be princes, nobles, judges, lesser rulers, and "the
saints of the most High" (Dan. 7:18; see also Isa.
32:1). He will rule with a rod of iron because within
His kingdom are enemies and persons who, having
been born during His righteous reign, yield only
feigned obedience (Pss. 2:9; 18:44 NASB marg.
note). When necessary, the rain will be withheld
from the disobedient, or they will be smitten with
the plague (Zech. 14:17-18). Otherwise, His rule will
be characterized by universal peace, joy, holiness,
and justice. "The earth shall be filled with the
knowledge of the glory of the LORD, as the waters
cover the sea" (Hab. 2:14).

In the world of nature, the curse will be removed
in measure, and trees will replace thorns and briers
(Isa. 55:13). Animal nature will be changed. Wild
beasts will become as they were before sin brought

violence and death into the world. Children will play with bears and serpents without fear, and lambs will play among presently dangerous creatures in perfect safety (Isa. 11:6-8). After the cataclysmic changes in the heavens and the earth that are to take place during the Tribulation and at the Lord's return, the light of the sun and the moon will be much greater (Isa. 30:26). Rivers and streams will break out everywhere, and rainfall will be plentiful, increasing the productivity of the land and making the desert bloom (Isa. 35:1-7). The unseen world of evil spirits will no longer dominate nations and wicked men, because Satan and his demons will be shut up in prison (Isa. 24:21-22; Rev. 20:1-3).

The life of people during the Kingdom age will be greatly prolonged, becoming comparable to the life of a tree (Isa. 65:21-22). Although death will still be present, the death of an individual at age 100 is likened to that of a child (Isa. 65:20). Sickness and deformity will be gone (Isa. 29:18; 33:24; 35:6). Old men and women will be seen in the streets, but the aging process is to continue; every man will walk "with his staff in his hand for very age" (Zech. 8:4). The institution of marriage will continue, and the joyful sounds of wedding parties will be heard again (Jer. 33:10-11).

In addition to the considerable revelation about general conditions among men everywhere, there are particular references to the blessings of the people of Israel under Messiah's rule. All Israel is to be saved (Rom. 11:26). Inasmuch as all wicked and rebellious Jews are to be purged out by the Lord after He regathers His people so that only the righteous will enter the land (Ezek. 20:33-42), this statement describes the situation at the dawn of the Kingdom.

After God gives each of His people a new heart and a new spirit, His law will be in their hearts. A supernatural enablement will bring to pass something similar to what the psalmist expressed when he wrote, "Thy word have I hid in mine heart, that I might not sin against thee" (Ps. 119:11). The Jews will be known and acknowledged among the Gentiles as the people whom God has blessed (Zech. 8:13). Whereas they were "a curse among the heathen" during the years of their dispersion, they are going to be a blessing, fulfilling the promise made to Abraham four thousand years ago, "Thou shalt be a blessing: . . . in thee shall all families of the earth be blessed" (Gen. 12:2-3).

The rapid multiplication of the Jewish people during the Kingdom age is a recurring theme of the prophets. This is set against an almost unbelievable destruction of both Jews and Gentiles during the Great Tribulation. The Lord said concerning that time, "Except those days should be shortened, there should no flesh be saved: but for the elect's sake those days shall be shortened" (Matt. 24:22). Some passages indicate this will be an actual shortening of the length of the day, when God shakes the heavens, and the earth moves out of her place (Isa. 13:13; Amos 8:9). Joel also raised the question whether mankind will be able to survive the terrors of the Tribulation: "The day of the LORD is great and very terrible; and who can abide it?" (Joel 2:11). A single verse in the book of Revelation mentions the killing of one third of the entire human race (Rev. 9:18).

An even more dreadful slaughter of the Jewish people living in Palestine at that time is described. "In all the land, saith the LORD, two parts therein shall be cut off and die; but the third shall be left therein. And I will bring the third part through the fire, and will refine them as silver is refined, and will try them as gold is tried" (Zech. 13:8-9).

Afterward, the Kingdom will witness a great increase in the number of Jews (Ezek. 36:37-38). Moses long ago promised that God would multiply His people above their fathers after the Lord returns (Deut. 30:5). Hosea repeated the promise: "Yet the number of the children of Israel shall be as the sand of the sea" (Hos. 1:10). God used this same figure of the sand of the sea in His words to Abraham (Gen. 22:17). The figure is used one final time, of when the enemies of the Lord and His people will have become so numerous that the number of them will be as the sand of the sea (Rev. 20:8). This will be just before their final destruction after the Kingdom has ended. During the Kingdom, "Israel shall blossom and bud, and fill the face of the world with fruit" (Isa. 27:6).

The promise has been given that the people of Israel will have beauty for ashes, the oil of joy for mourning, and the garment of praise for the spirit of heaviness. They will build the old wastes, raise up the former desolations, and repair the cities laid waste by the final conflict of Armageddon. Passages describing the peaceful life of those days contain striking details. Jews will employ Gentiles to feed their flocks, plow their fields, and dress their vineyards (Isa. 61:5). Prosperous as never before, Jewish people will "eat the riches of the Gentiles, and in their glory shall ye boast yourselves" (Isa. 61:6).

With the church gone from the earth, the Jews will be called the ministers of God, the Lord's witnesses, which implies the carrying on of a worldwide missionary enterprise (Isa. 43:10). It will originate in the land of Israel, and not in the Gentile nations as it does today. In those days people from other nations will seek out the Jews because they will know God is with them (Zech. 8:23). In the words of Moses, "The Lord shall make thee the head, and not the tail; and thou shalt be above only, and thou shalt not be beneath" (Deut. 28:13).

Just as God has fulfilled every word of the dark side of prophecy about Israel, He will also fulfill the bright side. The songs of bards and minstrels who have sung of past golden ages will be forgotten in the glory of the fulfillment of what the Hebrew prophets have written. Although these studies cannot explore the inexhaustible theme of Messianic prophecy, it is evident that there can be no Kingdom without a King, who is to be the Messiah, the Son of David.

God promised to David a family, a throne, and a kingdom forever in the great Davidic covenant, which incorporated a reference to chastening for iniquity (2 Sam. 7:10-16). This did not abrogate the promise, but it did anticipate the present age during which the people of Israel were to "abide many days without a king" (Hos. 3:4-5). Christians have believed for two thousand years that Israel's future king is going to be Jesus of Nazareth, vindicated and glorified before all intelligences in the same place where He was rejected and crucified. How this can be possible in the light of a curse pronounced on the royal line of King David is explained in the New Testament.

Jeconiah, or Coniah, was a wicked king in the Davidic line. His sin was so grievous that it was prophesied about him, "Thus saith the LORD, Write ye this man childless, a man that shall not prosper in his days: for no man of his seed shall prosper, sitting upon the throne of David, and ruling any more in Judah" (Jer. 22:30).

In Matthew 1 the genealogy is given of "Joseph the husband of Mary, of whom was born Jesus, who is called Christ." Jeconiah's name appears in the record, which means no descendant of his could ever be the Messiah, reigning on the throne of David. However, the problem is immediately solved by the use of language that makes it clear this is not a record of Mary's ancestors, and by the revelation that Mary was a virgin in whom the conception of Jesus was the work of the Holy Spirit, as Isaiah had prophesied (Isa. 7:14). It may be said that the legal title to the throne of David belonged to Joseph, but the first son born in his home was not his child. When the genealogy of Mary is given in Luke 3, Nathan, another son of David, is listed, rather than Solomon, ancestor of Jeconiah. Because of the doctrine of the virgin birth, the curse of Coniah has no bearing on the qualifications of Jesus of Nazareth as Israel's Messiah and King (Matt. 1:11, 18-25).

A question is sometimes raised about the relationship godly Jews from Old Testament days will sustain to the future Kingdom. It must be remembered that God's Word does not answer every question we might ask about future ages. We have been given "all things that pertain unto life and godliness" (2 Pet. 1:3), but not everything we might wish has been revealed to satisfy our curiosity. Nevertheless, it has pleased God to give us some information about the distant future, with which we must be satisfied until He gives us more.

It is clear that the Kingdom is going to be on the present earth, and that its subjects will be the righteous who survive the Tribulation period, both Jews and Gentiles. Those people will live their lives on this earth in that coming age, just as their ancestors lived their lives during preceding ages. All the Kingdom promises will be fulfilled at that time. It will be true again as it was during the ancient Jewish kingdom: "There hath not failed one word of all his good promise" (1 Kings 8:56). There will be a Jewish nation, ruled by the Messiah and blessed by God, in which every detail mentioned by the prophets will become historical fact.

Compared with the relatively small number of living persons who enter the Kingdom after the dreadful destruction of human beings during the Tribulation, the number of righteous people who died in previous ages must be very large. Two things were promised to them, resurrection and rewards (Dan. 12:2). Those who sleep in the dust of the earth will awake to everlasting life. Resurrection means they are to be given new bodies. Job said he expected to see God "in my flesh" in the latter day, beholding Him with his own eyes (Job 19:25-27). The psalmist recorded his own expectation: "I will behold thy face in righteousness: I shall be satisfied, when I awake, with thy likeness" (Ps. 17:15). Wrote Isaiah, "Awake

and sing, ye that dwell in dust: for thy dew is as the
dew of herbs, and the earth shall cast out the dead"
(Isa. 26:19).

The most complete description of the nature of
the resurrection body is given in the New Testament
(1 Cor. 15:35-53). It was written primarily about
what awaits the Christian, but it is certainly appli-
cable to Old Testament saints as well. It will be a
spiritual body, suited to life in the spirit in a new
environment, just as our present bodies are physical, suited to the life of the soul in the physical
world. Our present bodies are instruments by which
the soul is able to communicate with the material
world around us, while we move around in it. Our
new bodies will be instruments of the spirit, en-
abling us to become a part of the realm of the spirit.

It is written, "When he shall appear, we shall be
like him" (1 John 3:2). That means we will no longer
be subject to the natural laws of the material world.
We will be able, like the Lord in His resurrection
body, to pass through closed doors and appear to
others, as He did, and like Him to pass from one
place to another in a moment of time (John 20:17,
19). Many other facts about the bodies of resurrected persons are given in 1 Corinthians 15.

An examination of every passage in Scripture
dealing with the people of Israel after they are raised
from the dead discloses that nothing is said about
their residing on the present earth. It would be no
great marvel if they did move visibly among mortals
in the world because the Lord walked the earth for
forty days in His resurrection body. However, there
seems to be no statement in the Bible to the effect
that this will be the case.

The clearest light on where Old Testament men and women of faith will live after they rise from the dead is found in the book of Hebrews. Abraham "looked for a city which hath foundations, whose builder and maker is God" (Heb. 11:10). "These all died in faith, not having received the promises, but having seen them afar off, and were persuaded of them, and embraced them, and confessed that they were strangers and pilgrims on the earth. . . . they desire a better country, that is, an heavenly: wherefore God is not ashamed to be called their God: for he hath prepared for them a city" (Heb. 11:13-16).

What city is this, prepared by God for His ancient people? It is "the city of the living God, the heavenly Jerusalem," where we read of angels, the church, and "the spirits of just men made perfect" (Heb. 12:22-23). An extended description of it is given in Revelation 21:9-27. It descends out of heaven from God, illuminating the whole earth with its glory. Since it is not said to rest upon the earth, it is assumed that it is suspended above the earth. The names of the twelve tribes of the children of Israel are written on the twelve gates of the city. This heavenly city is what God has prepared as the residence of His faithful people who lived before the present age.

It seems to be a principle that the closer we come to eternity in the Bible, the briefer is the revelation we have been given. Instead of details about what life is going to be like, we are told only that the unhappy things of life in a world under the curse will be gone. "There shall be no more death, neither sorrow, nor crying, neither shall there be any more pain: for the former things are passed away. And he that sat upon the throne said, Behold, I make all things new" (Rev. 21:4-5). There is evidently no need for us to know more, doubtless because our understanding is too limited for us to be able to understand anything beyond what God has been pleased to reveal.

The resurrected people of Israel will share in the rule of the Kingdom. Of David it is specifically said, "They shall serve the LORD their God, and David their king, whom I will raise up unto them" (Jer. 30:9). Again, "I the LORD will be their God, and my servant David a prince among them; I the LORD have spoken it" (Ezek. 34:24). "I will be their God. And David my servant shall be king over them" (Ezek. 37:23-24).

Alongside this may be placed the words of the Lord in the New Testament: "Ye which have followed me, in the regeneration when the Son of man shall sit in the throne of his glory, ye also shall sit upon twelve thrones, judging the twelve tribes of Israel" (Matt. 19:28), fulfilling the promise, "I will restore thy judges as at the first," recorded in Isaiah 1:26.

Such passages are in perfect agreement with the parable of the nobleman who went to a far country to receive for himself a kingdom. When he returned, he gave authority over various cities to be his faithful servants (Luke 19:11-27). Additional truth is found in occasional brief promises: "If we suffer, we shall also reign with him" (2 Tim. 2:12); "we shall reign on the earth" (Rev. 5:10). We are not informed whether this is a visible reign or one like the present ministry of angels.

After the Kingdom has ended and eternity has dawned, Israel is going to continue as a distinct people throughout eternity. Any biblical doctrine of the eternal state must take two texts into consideration. "As the new heavens and the new earth, which I will make, shall remain before me, saith the LORD, so shall your seed and your name remain" (Isa. 66:22). "Thus saith the LORD, which giveth the sun for a light by day, and the ordinances of the moon and of the stars for a light by night . . . If those ordinances depart from before me, saith the LORD, then the seed of Israel also shall cease from being a nation before me for ever" (Jer. 31:35-37).

THE LAND OF PALESTINE

10

A Remarkable Land

Palestine is the only land ever given by God to any nation. How this came about is a story hardly known these days even to college graduates, although it is familiar enough to every Sunday school child. The Bible record is brief and simple. The first ten chapters are devoted to the history of the world and its people, covering perhaps two thousand years. Chapter 11 recounts the confounding of human language and the scattering of the race across the face of the earth. Then suddenly the Bible becomes the story of one man and his descendants.

God had spoken to Adam and his family, and again to Noah and his family at the time of the flood, but four hundred silent years passed before we read that He spoke again to a man on the earth. The genealogy of Genesis 11 indicates that about five hundred years passed from the birth of Shem to the call of Abram. At that time God said to Abram, "Get thee out of thy country, and from thy kindred, and from thy father's house, unto a land that I will shew thee" (Gen. 12:1). His home was in the city of Ur in southern Babylonia, on the Euphrates River, not far from the Persian Gulf.

In an act of faith at which men still marvel, Abram took his family from the home of their ancestors in the pagan land of Chaldea to begin a long journey of about six hundred miles up the Euphrates to a town called Haran. With him went his wife, Sarai; his brother's son Lot; and his father, Terah, who died in Haran. Abram was already seventy-five years old at that time.

After his father's death he traveled nearly four hundred miles south through the highlands of Canaan to a place called Shechem. There God appeared to him and said, "Unto thy seed will I give this land" (Gen. 12:7). At that moment Palestine became the promised land.

Dwelling in tents and moving about with his flocks and herds, Abram was encouraged occasionally by additional revelations of what God had in mind for his descendants. The gift of the land was eternally sure. "For all the land which thou seest, to thee will I give it, and to thy seed for ever" (Gen. 13:15). The promise was confirmed in "an everlasting covenant. . . . for an everlasting possession" (Gen. 17:7-8). In these passages the Hebrew word *olam* is used, meaning "to the end of days," or "for time out of mind," the nearest equivalent to our word *eternity*.

When Abram's son Isaac reached adulthood nearly one hundred years later, the promise was repeated to him. "Unto thee, and unto thy seed, I will give all these countries, and I will perform the oath which I sware unto Abraham thy father" (Gen. 26:3). After another seventy years Isaac's son Jacob had grown to manhood. God said to him, "The land which I gave Abraham and Isaac, to thee I will give it, and to thy seed after thee will I give the land" (Gen. 35:12). The Old Testament mentions this promise a number of times.

There could be no uncertainty about what land was in view. God Himself gave its boundaries, "from the river of Egypt unto the great river, the river Euphrates" (Gen. 15:18). This seems clear enough, but not everyone agrees on the meaning of the term "the river of Egypt." Many take it as a reference to the Nile because the same Hebrew word for "a flowing river" is used in the text for both streams. This seems to agree with Exodus 23:31. Others think the river of Egypt is identical with "the brook of Egypt," wrongly translated "the river of Egypt" several places in the King James Version of the Bible. The brook, or wadi, became the actual border of the land first occupied by the Jews under Joshua (Josh. 15:4; NASB).

The brook is usually identified today with the Wadi el-Arish, an intermittent torrent, dry during the summer, located on the Mediterranean coast some 50 miles south of Gaza and 140 miles from the Nile River. Students who insist on the verbal plenary view of the inspiration of the Scriptures are unwilling to grant that the river of Genesis 15:18 should be changed into a wadi for the sole reason that Israel's conquest of the land stopped at a wadi. This question becomes of great importance when the limits of the land in the kingdom and the future growth of the nation Israel are considered.

Every Bible in the world contains copies of these documents stating God's purpose to give a particu-

lar land to Israel in perpetuity. Scripture makes it
clear He had the right to do this. He is its Creator; He
said of this part of the world, "The land is mine"
(Lev. 25:23). The Bible also makes clear the principle that He would not long permit wickedness there
without judging its people. In Abram's day the wickedness of the Amorites who lived in the land was
"not yet full" (Gen. 15:16). When it reached the
place where a long-suffering God could no longer
tolerate it, He drove out the inhabitants to make way
for the Jewish people.

No other place in all the earth stands at such a
strategic spot. It forms the land bridge connecting
the continents of Europe, Asia, and Africa. Most of
the world's population is found on those three continents. The white, yellow, and black races meet
there in one geographic center. Their colors are
blended in such a way in Palestine that the native
population is described as olive skinned. No race
need feel it is excluded from the divine program
unfolding in the land of Israel from ancient times.

No better place could have been chosen for the
writing of the Bible and the sending forth of the
Word of God throughout the world. It was ideally
situated at the crossroads of the great ancient civilizations. Memphis, in the heart of Egypt, was only
250 miles away. The capital cities of Assyria and
Babylon were 500 miles to the northeast as the
crow flies.

Palestine is located at the center of the land surface of the globe. Ezekiel called it "the navel of the
earth" (Ezek. 38:12, ASV marg. note). Tourists in
Palestine today are told by their guides that the traditional spot where the cross of Calvary stood has

been called "the center of the earth" for centuries. Arab guides use the same expression when they show visitors the Dome of the Rock.

The Midrash Tanchuma, *Quedoshim* says of the Holy Land,

> As the navel is set in the center of the human body, so is the land of Israel the navel of the world . . . situated in the center of the world, and Jerusalem in the center of the land of Israel, and the sanctuary in the center of Jerusalem, and the holy place in the center of the sanctuary, and the ark in the center of the holy place, and the foundation stone before the holy place, because from it the world was founded. (The exposed rock over which the Dome of the Rock is built is called "the foundation stone.")

Located in the lower half of the eastern end of the Mediterranean, the traditional land Israel actually occupied is a strip only about one hundred forty miles long and forty-five miles wide, extending from Dan to Beersheba and from the Mediterranean to the hills east of the Jordan valley. It rises from a coastal plain to the hill country where Jerusalem stands, then falls away to the Jordan, thirteen hundred feet below sea level at the Dead Sea. To the east are mountains—those of Bashan in the north, Gilead in the center, and Moab in the south.

One can better understand the love of the Jews for their land after reading Moses' description of it.

> For the LORD thy God bringeth thee into a good land, a land of brooks of water, of fountains and depths that spring out of valleys and hills; a land of wheat, and barley, and vines, and fig trees, and pomegranates; a land of oil olive, and honey; a land

wherin thou shalt eat bread without scarceness, thou shalt not lack any thing in it; a land whose stones are iron, and out of whose hills thou mayest dig brass. When thou hast eaten and art full, then thou shalt bless the LORD thy God for the good land which he hath given thee (Deut. 8:7-10).

Again, "The land, whither ye go to possess it, is a land of hills and valleys, and drinketh water of the rain of heaven: a land which the LORD thy God careth for: the eyes of the LORD thy God are always upon it, from the beginning of the year even unto the end of the year" (Deut. 11:11-12).

Everyone can feel a familiarity with Palestine because it is similar to many other lands. The natural features of all lands are found there. There are mountains, deserts, seacoasts, interior plains, snow-capped peaks, and the lowest valley in the world. There are grazing lands, farmlands, volcanic wastes, barren places, and fruitful places. Native to the country are palm trees, pine trees, cedars, fruit trees, and shade trees. The climate varies from temperate to tropical. Some snow falls in the hill country in the winter.

Nowhere else in the world is there a larger variety of animals similar to those found in other regions of the earth. There are, or were, bears, gazelles, wolves, dogs, camels, leopards, lions, foxes, wild boars, hares, squirrels, deer, buffalo, oxen, sheep, goats, and desert monitors. Naturalists also list chameleons, tortoises, frogs, snakes, butterflys, and mosquitoes. More than three hundred species of birds sing in the trees. Men of all climes find something here to remind them of home.

The different names applied to Palestine in Scripture are of great interest. It is the land of Canaan, the Holy Land, and the land of Jordan, the glorious land, Jehovah's land, the glory of all lands, and Immanuel's land. Eighteen times it is called the land flowing with milk and honey, making this the most common designation. Three names link it to the nation to which God gave it: the land of the Hebrews, the land of Israel, and land of the Jews (Gen. 40:15; Matt. 2:20; Acts 10:39). The name *Palestine* appears once; *Palestina*, three times (Exod. 15:14; Isa. 14:29, 31; Joel 3:4). This name has become widely used, appearing on the maps of millions of copies of the Bible, but it is of Greek and Roman—not biblical—origin, and it is changed to *Philistia* in the revised and other versions.

America has always owed a debt to Palestine because it became, under a Scripture meant for Israel, the first land of liberty known to history. The text of Scripture placed on the Liberty Bell was a passage about the land of Israel: "Proclaim liberty throughout all the land unto all the inhabitants thereof" (Lev. 25:10). Christian students of history are convinced that any land which seeks to honor the God of the Bible, as the United States has done in the past, receives His blessing and prospers.

The land is referred to in the Old Testament some fifteen hundred times. It appears frequently in the gospels and Acts in connection with the earthly life of Jesus of Nazareth and the movements of the disciples in the early church. The land is scarcely mentioned in the epistles, and then only with reference to Abraham and the people of Israel (Heb. 11:9, 15). Passages having to do with the church and its destiny contain no references to the land.

This is in perfect keeping with the revealed purposes of God. The church is a heavenly people rather than an earthly one. It has no relationship to the land except that it began there.

Individuals being called out from mankind as the children of God during the present age are "partakers of the heavenly calling" (Heb. 3:1). Their inheritance is reserved in heaven. All their blessings are in heavenly places (Eph. 1:3), or "the heavenlies." When the Lord comes someday to take His church away from the world He will not come to the land, or even to the earth. He will come instead to the air to call all believers to Himself, to be with Him forever (1 Thess. 4:17).

11

Tragedy Follows Blessing

From the time of Abraham to the Babylonian captivity, the Bible is primarily a history of the Jewish people, but there are also some seven hundred fifty references to the land in those pages. Many of them are of great importance.

Under the leadership of Joshua the Jews drove out the evil inhabitants of Palestine. God gave them strange allies to make their task easier. He said,

> I will send hornets before thee, which shall drive out the Hivite, the Canaanite, and the Hittite, from before thee. I will not drive them out from before thee in one year; lest the land become desolate, and the beast of the field multiply against thee. By little and little I will drive them out from before thee, until thou be increased, and inherit the land (Exod. 23:28-29).

When twelve men were sent in to search out Canaan they discovered something of its astonishing productivity. Arriving in Hebron, "they came unto the brook of Eshcol, and cut down from thence a branch with one cluster of grapes, and they bare it between two upon a staff; and they brought of the pomegranates, and of the figs" (Num. 13:23). In our own day the size and quality of the produce of the land are often remarkable. Sugar beets may weigh forty pounds. Some of the fruit is considered the best in the world.

Many exploits of the Jews during the conquest of Canaan are very well known. Representative of those that still inspire the people of God is the instructive story of how Caleb secured his inheritance. He had seen the sons of Anak dwelling in Hebron during his exploration of the area. They were of such gigantic stature that he and his friends reported, "We were in our own sight as grasshoppers, and so we were in their sight" (Num. 13:33). Now eighty-five years of age, Caleb was confident he could win the victory over these giants because he had wholly followed the Lord. He said to Joshua, "Give me this mountain . . . I shall be able to drive them out as the LORD said" (Josh. 14:12). By faith he overcame them, and "Hebron therefore became the inheritance of Caleb" (Josh. 14:14).

After the land was conquered it was divided among the tribes by lot. Containing cities already built and vineyards already planted, it became to the Jews "the land of your possession," the inheritance God had promised. Thereafter it is frequently referred to in Scripture as Israel's inheritance (Deut. 15:4; 1 Chron. 16:18). The same designation is used when the land is divided among the tribes at the beginning of the Kingdom age (Ezek. 48:29). The language is always consistent; never is the church said to have any inheritance except a heavenly one.

Because God was favorable to the land, it yielded its increase. There His people found safety and peace. When war became necessary the Lord gave them victory over their enemies. They multiplied and became a great nation. They were so closely associated with the land as their inheritance that even the land was tithed, and the tithe belonged to the Lord. The fields were sown for six years, then permitted to rest for one year (Lev. 25:1-4). When this commandment was disobeyed for a period of 490 years, God removed the Jews "until the land had enjoyed her sabbaths: for as long as she lay desolate she kept sabbath, to fulfil threescore and ten years" (2 Chron. 36:20-21). The length of the captivity was determined by the number of years the land had been neglected.

During all the years when the Lord dwelt among His people, the Shekinah glory was present in the land, first in the tabernacle and then in the temple. It was visible between the cherubim above the Mercy Seat of the Ark, manifesting the presence of the Lord. In the Holy Land Jesus of Nazareth was born, lived, died, and was raised from the dead. From the land He ascended to heaven, and to it He will return to deliver Jerusalem and His people from the most terrible war in their long history. The church began in Palestine when the Holy Spirit descended from heaven to take up His residence in His new temple, made up of all people who put their trust in the Lord during the present age. From the promised land has come our Bible.

Palestine is revered by millions as the holy land of the three great monotheistic religions, Christianity, Judaism, and Muhammadanism. It has been a place for religious pilgrimages over the centuries, as Moses predicted (Deut. 29:22). Here the battle of Armageddon is to take place, in the Plain of Esdraelon, which Napoleon called the world's greatest battlefield. The land will become the graveyard of many nations and the scene of the judgment of the Gentiles. It is destined finally to become the seat of world government under the Messiah.

From the beginning, Israel's fortunes have been inseparably linked to the land. God said, "If ye walk in my statutes, and keep my commandments, and do them; then I will give you rain in due season, and the land shall yield her increase, and the trees of the field shall yield their fruit" (Lev. 26:3-4). Set over against this promise were warnings about the results of disobedience. "I will make your heaven as iron, and your earth as brass: and your strength shall be spent in vain: for your land shall not yield her increase, neither shall the trees of the land yield their fruits. . . . And I will bring the land into desolation" (Lev. 26:19-20,32).

The Old Testament is filled with evidence of the accuracy of these statements. As the centuries passed, Palestine was indeed a fruitful land, filled with cattle and flocks of sheep. Wealth accumulated. Gold and silver were commonplace during the reign of Solomon. The land supported a population of millions of Jews. Forests were found everywhere, such as those of Lebanon, Ephraim, and Carmel. Thirty-five hundred species of plants exist in Palestine, of which one hundred are named in the Bible.

Nevertheless, this rich land lost its people. The language used to describe what happened is quite remarkable. "Ye shall therefore keep my statutes and my judgments . . . that the land spue not you out also, when ye defile it, as it spued out the nations that were before you" (Lev. 18:26-28). Jeremiah wrote, "Thus saith the LORD, Behold, I will sling out the inhabitants of the land" (Jer. 10:18).

The desolation of the land began before the captivities took place. Moses had warned of the curses to come if the people ceased to hearken to the voice of the Lord their God: "Thy heaven that is over thy head shall be brass, and the earth that is under thee shall be iron. The LORD shall make the rain of thy land powder and dust" (Deut. 28:23-24). When Elijah the prophet announced the coming of an extended drought because of wickedness, the basis of his warning was this word given through Moses. Elijah announced, "As the LORD God of Israel liveth, before whom I stand, there shall not be dew nor rain these years, but according to my word" (1 Kings 17:1). The same thing was said by Haggai: "Therefore the heaven over you is stayed from dew, and the earth is stayed from her fruit. And I called for a drought upon the land" (Hag. 1:10-11).

Jeremiah wrote a terrible prophecy of the tragic fate of the land. Then he asked: Who will be wise enough to understand why "the land perisheth and is burned up like a wilderness, that none passeth through? And the LORD said, Because they have forsaken my law which I set before them, and have not obeyed my voice, neither walked therein" (Jer. 9:12-13). With a broken heart he said, "The land is full of adulterers; for because of swearing the land mourneth; the pleasant places of the wilderness are dried up" (Jer. 23:10). The Lord said further through Ezekiel, "The land is full of bloody crimes, and the city is full of violence. . . . I will do unto them after their way, and according to their deserts will I judge them; and they shall know that I am the LORD" (Ezek. 7:23,27).

The record is almost unbelievably sad. Worms ate the vineyards of Israel. Locusts destroyed the vegetation, and olive trees cast their fruit. God sent the sword, the famine, and the pestilence among the people until they were consumed from off the land He had given them. The songs that had filled the homes of the Jews in their promised land ceased. No longer did the voice of rejoicing and salvation fill the tabernacles of the righteous. They asked, "How shall we sing the LORD'S song in a strange land?" (Ps. 137:4).

No one could claim the people had not been warned. They were told specifically, "There shall be no grapes on the vine, nor figs on the fig tree, and the leaf shall fade" (Jer. 8:13). "There shall come up briers and thorns" (Isa. 5:6). The land was described as in mourning, the herbs of every field withered, because of the wickedness of those who dwelt within its borders (Jer. 12:4). Its Creator speaks of the land as though it were a living thing: "They have made it desolate, and being desolate it mourneth unto me" (Jer. 12:11).

Evil leadership was one of the kinds of wickedness that brought the judgment of a holy God on Palestine. Kings like Saul and Ahab "troubled the land." Homosexuality was permitted, and it increased. "There were also sodomites in the land: and they did according to all the abominations of the nations which the LORD cast out before the children of Israel" (1 Kings 14:24). The people were involved with the occult, absolutely forbidden by the God of Israel. Even King Manasseh "dealt with familiar spirits and wizards: he wrought much wickedness in the sight of the LORD" (2 Kings 21:6). The land became filled with physical violence. Wrote the psalmist, "I have seen violence and strife in the city" (Ps. 55:9). Prophecy reveals that these same evils are to become as prominent in the world of the last days as they were in the land of Israel prior to the captivities.

There was no message from God during the 400 years before Abraham was told to enter the land. A similar period of 400 years of silence followed the return of the remnant after they had been removed from Palestine. Certain facts can be learned about the Jews and their land from secular history during that period, but no divine revelation was given between Malachi, last of the postcaptivity prophets, and Matthew.

When New Testament history began, a godly remnant existed in the land among the descendants of the exiles who returned from Babylon. Palestine was under the control of the Roman Empire, whose people were destined to destroy Jerusalem in accordance with Daniel's prophecy. The throne was occupied by Herod, an Edomite. The magnificent temple he had constructed knew nothing of the Shekinah glory. Because of the judgment of God, the land had changed little since Old Testament days. We read of desert places, wilderness, dearth and famine, disease and misery, violence and death. There was widespread satanic and demonic activity.

Among the faithful there was a general expectation of the coming of the Messiah. Records had been kept carefully by which He could be identified, although such genealogies were destroyed in A.D. 70, after the ancestry of Jesus of Nazareth had been prepared. The priesthood had become corrupt, but scholarly scribes carefully preserved the Scriptures.

Early in the New Testament it is stated that with the beginning of the preaching of Jesus of Nazareth the words of the prophet Isaiah were fulfilled: "The people which sat in darkness saw great light; and to them which sat in the region and shadow of death light is sprung up" (Matt. 4:16). Shepherds saw the glory of the Lord at the time of the birth of Jesus (Luke 2:8-9). God began once more to speak from heaven. The men were already living in the land through whom God was once more to give His written Word to the world.

As before, good news was mingled with warnings of judgment. "Whosoever shall not receive you, nor hear your words, when ye depart out of that house or city, shake off the dust of your feet. Verily I say unto you, it shall be more tolerable for the land of Sodom and Gomorrha in the day of judgment, than for that city" (Matt. 10:14-15). The new message from the Lord could hardly have been given more solemn importance, but it was afterward revealed that the persistent rejection of the good news God had given concerning His Son is an unpardonable sin. Thus the unpardonable sin is the rejection of God's one great sacrifice for sin, toward which every blood sacrifice offered in the land for centuries had pointed.

The most deeply moving reference to the land in all the New Testament is found in Matthew 27:45-

46. "Now from the sixth hour there was darkness over all the land unto the ninth hour. And about the ninth hour Jesus cried with a loud voice, saying, Eli, Eli, lama sabachthani? that is to say, My God, my God, why hast thou forsaken me?" This terrible cry and the darkness during which it was uttered are found in the opening verses of the Messianic 22d Psalm. Then the reason is given why the Son of God was forsaken in that hour of agony. His cry was not heard because, as the psalmist prophetically said of Him, "I am a worm, and no man" (Ps. 22:6).

The astonishing truth is that the word translated "worm" is the Hebrew *towlath*, a tiny creature of the land of Palestine which, like the cochineal insect, was crushed to produce the scarlet color used to dye the priest's garments (Exod. 28:5), and used in such ordinances as that of the red heifer and the two birds (Lev. 14:4; Num. 19:6). The Lord had become a *towlath*. His blood was being shed in payment for all the sins covered by the blood of bulls and goats ever since the sacrificial system was inaugurated at the Garden of Eden. His blood had been symbolized for centuries by the crimson color of the *towlath*.

12

In the Latter Days

It is sometimes said that prophecy is being fulfilled in Palestine every day, but no conservative student of Scripture would agree. When the return of
large numbers of Jewish people is cited as proof
that the predicted divine restoration has begun, it
need only be pointed out that the Lord is not going
to regather and restore His people until after His
return to the earth. It is indeed an impressive historical event that the land is so heavily populated by
Jews that an Israeli nation has come into being after
nineteen centuries during which this seemed impossible. Seen in its proper perspective, however,
and with due regard to what the Bible actually says,
this is rather a movement in the direction of what
the prophets indicate is to be a Jewish population in
the land in the latter days, before the Lord returns.

Guides who conduct parties of tourists through
Palestine often comment, "See how the desert is
blossoming as the rose, as the Bible predicts!" The
productivity of the land since it began to be oc-

cupied by its ancient owners has certainly been astonishing, but this is a far cry from Isaiah's description of the Messianic Kingdom. The desert will blossom at that time, but the eyes of the blind will also be opened, the ears of the deaf will be unstopped, and the lame man will leap like a hart (Isa. 35:1-6). To point this out is not to deny to godly Jews their conviction that the hand of Israel's God has been on the land ever since its people began to drain swamps, use modern agricultural methods, and fertilize and irrigate the barren ground.

It is a scriptural principle that the land will yield its fruit only to the people who belong there, who have been given the land by the Lord, whose absence is the reason Palestine has been desolate for so long. Ezekiel wrote, "O mountains of Israel, ye shall shoot forth your branches, and yield your fruit to my people of Israel; for they are at hand to come" (Ezek. 36:8). The Jews have planted scores of millions of trees in places where no one thought anything could grow. In some areas hills that had been barren and stony for centuries are now clothed with dense forests as far as the eye can see. Where hardly a blade of grass grew before, valleys began to be covered with lush vegetation soon after Jewish people moved in. There can be no doubt that the land is responding to the loving care of its ancient people. Some students believe there is prophetic significance in Ezekiel's statement that the mountains of Israel will yield their fruit to the Jews when they are "at hand to come," that is, just prior to their restoration. On the other hand, there are conservative Jewish leaders in Palestine today who actually oppose the state of Israel because they insist that only the Messiah can bring about any of the glories predicted for the Messianic age.

Obviously, many things have taken place in Palestine in recent years that have led even secular columnists and newsmen to say they discern the activity of the God of Israel. Military victories, remarkable progress in many fields of endeavor, and the attention of the whole world have excited this kind of comment.

The writer had an interesting experience in Jerusalem a few years ago that illustrates the widespread interest in finding possible fulfillments of prophecy. A young Jewish guide said, "Did you know the Bible predicted modern archaeology?" To prove his point he turned to Psalm 102:13-14 and read, "Thou shalt arise, and have mercy upon Zion: for the time to favour her, yea, the set time, is come. For thy servants take pleasure in her stones, and favour the dust thereof." Then he said, "This is precisely what the archaeologists are doing. They are delighted with the stones they dig up, and they carefully screen the dust to find artifacts."

One of the best stories to come out of the land tells of a group of American tourists who were traveling in a desolate area. One of them said, "So this is what the Bible calls the land of milk and honey! I never saw such a sick land, with its burning heat and barren ground. There is hardly a blade of grass anywhere."

Another member of the group replied, "You have just fulfilled a prophecy found in the Bible you are criticizing." He opened the book of Deuteronomy and read these words: "The stranger that shall come from a far land, shall say, when they see the plagues of that land, and the sicknesses which the LORD hath laid upon it . . . the whole land therof is brimstone, and salt, and burning, that it is not sown, nor beareth, nor any grass groweth therein" (Deut. 29:22-23).

While visitors are being told by their guides of prophecies now being fulfilled, they are seeing evidence of the solemn truth of Ezekiel's words, even after twenty-five hundred years have passed: "Their holy places shall be defiled" (Ezek. 7:24). The holiest place in all Israel, the site of Solomon's temple, is occupied by the Muslim shrine known as the Mosque of Omar.

Every Bible encyclopedia and dictionary contains an article about Palestine, supplying information about the history and topography of the country. Yet it is almost impossible to find even a brief reference to the future of the land as it is set forth in Scripture. This is in spite of the fact that God has given us a considerable revelation. Prophecies dealing with the last days and the establishing of the kingdom tell us a great deal about what is going to happen to the land and its people. The land is mentioned ten times in Joel, twelve times in Zechariah, and thirty-three times in Ezekiel in passages having to do with the end times.

Chapters 38 and 39 of Ezekiel give an extended description of events said to take place in the latter years, or the latter days, preceding the kingdom described in the concluding chapters. The land itself is mentioned fifteen times. There are references to the mountains of Israel and its fields, forests, and villages. We read about such creatures as the fish, fowl, and beasts of the land. Natural forces come into play like hail, rain, and an earthquake severe enough to throw down mountains and steep places (Ezek. 38:20).

This extended passage deserves attention in any discussion of Palestine in the last days, even though students are not in agreement about just where the events of these chapters are to be placed in the chronology of the period. Certain facts are evident from a reading of the text. At the time those things take place there is a population of Jewish people in the land who have gathered together out of the nations. They live safely in cities unlike those known in the days of Ezekiel because they have no walls, bars, or gates. A great world power exists in the far north, unfriendly to Israel.

The Jews are prosperous enough to excite the greed of neighboring peoples who invade the land "to carry away silver and gold, to take away cattle and goods, to take a great spoil" (Ezek. 38:13). The presence of those enemy nations makes it clear that the Lord has not yet established His kingdom, which calls for casting out all wicked people from the earth. Furthermore, the divine regathering of all Israel, their restoration to the land, and the outpouring of the Holy Spirit do not take place until after the events of these chapters have transpired. Israel is not yet in the land under the blessing of God. The Jews do not come to know the Lord as their God until after the day when He intervenes to deliver them from the invading armies.

The prophecy begins, "Son of man, set your face toward Gog of the land of Magog, the prince of Rosh, Meshech, and Tubal, and prophesy against him" (Ezek. 38:2, NASB). (Some versions render "prince of Rosh" as "chief prince," but the ancient Septuagint and other versions translate the Hebrew *Rosh* as a proper name.) Among the efforts to identify this prince of Rosh, one is of special interest. In the ninth century the Byzantine Empire was invaded by barbarians from the north. Photius, patriarch of Constantinople, knew prophecy. He assumed the barbarians were the invaders of whom Ezekiel wrote, and called them Ros. The name became popular, passed from the Greek into the Russian language, underwent a change in spelling; and the land of these people from the north came to be known as Rucia, or Russia. Some Russian scholars are among those who believe this is the true origin of the name of that country.

We thus are faced with the astonishing fact that Ezekiel named a country that did not appear on the roll of the nations until more than fourteen hundred years later, when it was mentioned for the first time in a document dated A.D. 839. It would seem that God has branded, as it were, a great modern nation with the name He gave it in His Word many centuries earlier, when only a few scattered tribes occupied the desolate reaches far to the north of Palestine. Moscow is directly north of Jerusalem.

The several nations associated with Rosh in the invasion include countries of Europe, the Middle East, and North Africa. Five times the prophet says there will be "many people" with those nations. Since other areas of the world are specifically mentioned in prophecy, the source of those many people may be the Far East.

Certain problems are presented by this twenty-five hundred year-old document when it is studied

as an accurate description of events taking place in
the latter years. One of the problems arises from
what is said about the weaponry of the invading
armies. We read not only of horses but also of bows
and arrows. This has led to speculation about how
such terminology can be explained. The explanation may be very simple. Hebrew is a picture language; each noun is a word picture, a terse description. For example, a fox is literally "a burrower" in
Hebrew; a dog is "a barker"; a sparrow is "a hop-
per"; a serpent, "a hisser." A palm tree is "the erect
one," the sun, "the shining one." Comparable descriptive words in English are rare. They include
terms such as woodpecker, flyer, and flamethrower.

The horses of Ezekiel are, literally, "leapers." The
same word is used elsewhere of birds. It describes
something that propels itself rapidly over the
ground or through the air. This was the ordinary
term for a horse to the Hebrews, but that does not
mean it must be so translated in a description of the
latter years. The word could be used of a piece of
military equipment. Wheeled vehicles do appear in
Ezekiel 39:20. A sword was a cutting or destroying
instrument. An arrow was a piercing missile; a bow
was a device for launching such a missile.

Many versions of the Bible translate Ezekiel 39:3,
"And I will smite thy bow out of thy left hand, and
will cause thine arrows to fall out of thy right hand."
If we translate the verse by using word pictures instead of the ancient meanings they conveyed in the
prophet's day, it reads, "And I will smite thy launching device out of thy left hand, and will cause thy
missiles to fall out of thy right hand." Bows of wood
were used in Ezekiel's day, but again, there is no

compelling reason to render the Hebrew word according to the context of Ezekiel's day in a description of the latter days.

"After many days" the forces under the leadership of Rosh come into the land of Palestine. It might be supposed that Jewish armies would resist the attack with the help of allies, but no war or battle is mentioned in the text. Instead, the fury of Israel's God will be aroused, and He will intervene to destroy the invaders. He will hurl five ancient weapons against the forces of Rosh, divine weapons He used on behalf of the Jews in their early history.

The first weapon is to be an earthquake. A great shaking in Palestine will throw mountains and steep places down. Every wall will fall. In the days of Saul, Jonathan defeated the Philistines with the help of an earthquake (1 Sam. 14:15-23). The second weapon will be confusion within the enemy ranks, so great that "every man's sword shall be against his brother" (Ezek. 38:21). The same remarkable occurrence took place when Gideon destroyed the armies of Midian (Judg. 7:22).

When Jerusalem was under attack in the reign of Hezekiah, 185,000 soldiers in the Assyrian army were killed by pestilence in one night (2 Kings 19:35). God is going to use pestilence again against Rosh. The fourth weapon is to be "an overflowing rain, and great hailstones." The Bible speaks of hailstones weighing as much as one hundred pounds each. The destructive power of hail was seen in the victory of Gideon during Joshua's conquest of Canaan (Josh. 10:11). The fifth weapon will be fire and brimstone, used to defend Elijah, and reminding us of the destruction of Sodom and Gomorrah (2 Kings 1:10; Gen. 19:24).

The absence of any mention of war suggests an act of God so sudden that the invading armies will fall upon the mountains in the north of Israel before a defense can be organized. The text speaks of people going forth out of the cities to collect the military equipment left by the enemy, as though the invaders will never reach the densely populated areas.

The five divine weapons seem to be related. Earthquake and fire from the sky together can mean volcanic action. Rain with great hailstones could cause confusion and chaos among the armies. Pestilence of an unknown kind from an unidentified source has struck with deadly swiftness more than once in Palestine in ancient times. The word itself is used nearly fifty times in the Old Testament.

Russia, or Rosh, which has disturbed the peace of millions and has made the nations of the earth to tremble, will be destroyed so utterly that the world will stand aghast at what has happened. The awful words of God are, "I will turn thee back, and leave but the sixth part of thee. . . . Thou shalt fall upon the mountains of Israel. . . . Thou shalt fall upon the open field: for I have spoken it, saith the Lord GOD" (Ezek. 39:2-5). At the same time the armies are destroyed, fire is sent on Magog, the land from which many of them have come (Ezek. 39:6).

The magnitude of this disaster is almost incomprehensible. It will take the house of Israel seven months to bury the dead. The corpses and bones are to be deposited in a valley somewhere in Israel that will be called "the valley of Hamon-gog," or "the multitude of Gog." The Septuagint contains a statement to the effect that the burial valley is to be closed off with a wall. The care with which scattered bones of the dead are marked, then buried by special burial crews, has raised the question whether atomic radiation may not be involved in the catastrophe. Vast numbers of scavenger birds and beasts will gather to feed on the flesh of the men and animals of the invading confederacy. The "weapons," or, literally, "military equipment" discarded in the mountains will provide the people of the cities of Israel with fuel sufficient to last seven years.

The effect of what happens in Palestine will be worldwide, as the northern powers that came to take a spoil will find instead a place of graves. Four times the text mentions that the heathen, or nations, will know that Israel's God is the Lord. In fact, it is specifically declared that God "will bring thee against my land, that the heathen may know me" (Ezek. 38:16). Peter wrote, "The Lord is . . . not willing that any should perish, but that all should come to repentance" (2 Pet. 3:9). It seems clear that God will bring about the destruction of a great atheistic nation expressly to bring to pass the salvation of people in other nations all over the earth. It is revealed elsewhere that "a great multitude" from all nations is to come out of the Tribulation "washed . . . in the blood of the Lamb" (Rev. 7:9-14).

The text also emphasizes, "The house of Israel shall know that I am the LORD their God from that day and forward" (Ezek. 39:22). The chronology of this invasion by Rosh is obscure, so that it is not possible to settle finally the question of just when in the latter days such things happen. Nevertheless, these chapters of Ezekiel may describe the definitive event that brings about what Moses predicted, a return to the Lord by scattered Israel prior to the return of the Lord to regather them and restore them to their own land (Deut. 30:1-3).

Ezekiel's prophecy concludes with a description, introduced by the time word *Now*, of the divine gathering of the Jews "out of their enemies' lands" and into their own land. The Lord says, "I have gathered them unto their own land, and have left none of them any more there." He will pour out His Spirit on the house of Israel. Never again will He hide His face from them (Ezek. 39:25-29).

Here are two chapters of prophecy indicating that the land of Israel is going to command world attention in the last days. It will be at a time when a powerful, unprincipled, warlike nation will have risen in the north, manifesting enmity toward the Jews. This nation called Rosh by the prophet Ezekiel is unknown to Bible history except here. It is to be destroyed by a holy God for acts perpetrated against the land and people He has always called His own. The prophecy corresponds well with other Scriptures dealing with the purposes of God in the end times.

When we take these chapters literally we have an astonishing picture of events that could fit into the world as we know it today. Since this is the case, we ought not to be perplexed by a degree of difficulty in our understanding of some parts of the text. For a document more than twenty-five hundred years old, it is surprisingly easy to read and comprehend.

13

At the Lord's Return

The eyes of the Lord have always been on the land, even during the centuries when it lay barren and waste after its people were taken away (Deut. 11:12). He looks on it today, when great numbers of His chosen people have returned without having returned to Him. He has told us of His plans. The God who said, "I will bring the land into desolation" (Lev. 26:32), also said, "I will remember the land" (Lev. 26:42). He has given His promise, "I will cause to return the captivity of the land, as at the first, saith the LORD" (Jer. 33:11). This is the same Hebrew idiom Moses used of the people when he wrote, "The LORD thy God will turn thy captivity" (Deut. 30:3). Just as the people are to experience a deliverance from their centuries of trouble when they return to the Lord and obey His words, so the land is also going to be delivered.

When the day of the Lord comes, all nations will gather in the land to battle against Jerusalem (Zech. 14:2). The people of the city will face destruction.

This will be no ordinary invasion; a great turning point in history will have arrived. God will have brought to pass everything revealed in His Word that must precede the return of the Lord. There will be alarm in the land as the day approaches. The horn will be blown to warn and to assemble the Jews (Joel 2:1,15). The priests in the temple will weep as they pray, "Spare thy people, O LORD, and give not thine heritage to reproach, that the heathen should rule over them: wherefore should they say among the people, Where is their God?" (Joel 2:17).

The cry will rise to heaven, "Oh that thou wouldest rend the heavens, that thou wouldest come down, that the mountains might flow down at thy presence" (Isa. 64:1). As the people pray, the land itself will mourn to the Lord (Jer. 12:11), bespeaking the age-old condition of divine judgment described in the words, "The whole creation groaneth and travaileth in pain together until now" (Rom. 8:22). When Israel's cry reaches the ears of God at this strategic time during the latter days, it is written, "Then will the LORD be jealous for his land, and pity his people" (Joel 2:18). The reassuring words will be spoken, "Fear not, O land; be glad and rejoice: for the LORD will do great things" (Joel 2:21).

The transformation of Palestine into the glorious place it is to be during the Kingdom age is not going to result from gradual improvements by its inhabitants. It will begin with a physical disturbance so violent that it changes the appearance of the land altogether. As Zechariah tells us, all nations will gather against Jerusalem to battle. Half of the people will be taken captive, the city will fall, the houses will be rifled, and the women will be ravished.

> Then shall the LORD go forth, and fight against
> those nations, as when he fought in the day of
> battle. And his feet shall stand in that day upon the
> mount of Olives, which is before Jerusalem on the
> east, and the mount of Olives shall cleave in the
> midst thereof toward the east and toward the west,
> and there shall be a very great valley; and half of the
> mountain shall remove toward the north, and half
> of it toward the south (Zech. 14:3-4).

The Mount of Olives stands on a branch of the
Great Rift, an awesome cleavage, or fault line, in the
earth's crust extending more than three thousand
miles from the Jordan valley all the way to southeast
Africa. The famous Rift Valley lies in this crack in the
earth, as do the Red Sea, the Gulf of Aqaba, the
Dead Sea, and the valley of the Jordan. The fault
line is an earthquake zone.

A number of earthquakes in the land are mentioned in Scripture. The prophecy of Amos is dated
from one of them. An earthquake occurred at the
Crucifixion, and another at the resurrection. One is
mentioned in Acts. In 1927 Jerusalem was shaken
so badly that the Church of the Holy Sepulchre had
to be supported with scaffolding for many years to
keep it from falling. There are building restrictions
on the Mount of Olives today because geologists
have warned of the great danger of earthquakes
there.

Severe earthquakes are predicted for the last
days. Earthdwellers will hide in holes and caves for
fear of the Lord "when he ariseth to shake terribly
the earth" (Isa. 2:19). The greatest earthquake since
men have been on earth is yet to take place (Rev.
16:18). When the Lord goes forth from heaven to

deliver His people and His land, and His feet stand on the Mount of Olives, the effect will be that of a great earthquake. The mount will split open in the middle, producing a great valley. Visitors to Jerusalem today can actually see a depression in the middle of the mount, running east and west. It is visible in pictures of Olivet taken from the courtyard of the Dome of the Rock. A road lies in the depression, passing the Garden of Gethsemane and crossing the mount to Bethel on the other side. The depression is believed to mark an ancient line of cleavage.

When the prophet Zechariah described the valley created by the cleaving of the mount, he used a word picture of a deep valley with lofty sides. Joel, on the other hand, used another word picture emphasizing its broad spaciousness as he spoke of a valley in a similar context dealing with the latter day (Joel 3:2). Joel called it the valley of Jehoshaphat, a term occurring only in his prophecy. The word means "Jehovah judges." In that place the Lord is going to judge the nations He has gathered together.

Ever since the fourth century the small Valley of the Kidron, lying between Jerusalem and the Mount of Olives, has mistakenly been called Jehoshaphat. Some have therefore assumed this is where the Lord is going to sit in judgment, but there is no biblical basis for such an idea. The most likely place is the great valley created at the return of the Lord. It fits the language used by Joel, and it seems to be large enough for such a judgment scene as both he and Matthew described, when the nations will appear before the Lord and be judged on the basis of the way they have treated the Jews (Matt. 25:31-45).

The new valley is to become the way of escape for the besieged inhabitants of Jerusalem. They will flee as they "fled from before the earthquake in the days of Uzziah king of Judah" (Zech. 14:5). With the sun obscured, it will be a day of darkness, but it will be a day of deliverance (Zech. 12:5-6). The New Testament provides an interesting sidelight on the prophecy. Standing near the Mount of Olives, the Lord said, "If ye have faith as a grain of mustard seed, ye shall say unto this mountain, Remove hence to yonder place; and it shall remove" (Matt. 17:20). In accordance with the principle that prophecy is sometimes fulfilled in answer to the prayers of God's people, it is possible that this statement, often spiritualized to make it read, "mountain of difficulty," will be taken literally by believing Jews during the siege of Jerusalem. If so, the prayer of faith will precede the splitting of the mount and the moving of the halves northward and southward. The removal of a mountain may never have been necessary in the accomplishing of the will of God in the past, but He is going to move a mountain for His people in the last days.

Another tremendous physical change in Palestine will result from the same geological disturbance. "All the land shall be turned as a plain from Geba to Rimmon south of Jerusalem" (Zech. 14:10). This is parallel to Isaiah's prophecy, "The mountains shall depart, and the hills be removed" (Isa. 54:10). There will still be mountainous areas in other parts of the land, but a wide region that extends from south of Jerusalem to several miles north of the city will become flat instead of rugged and hilly, as it has al-

ways been in the past. Geba was six miles to the
north of Jerusalem, Rimmon thirty miles to the
south.

At the same time that the land in central Palestine
is leveled, the city of Jerusalem will be thrust upward to a commanding height (Zech. 14:10). During the Kingdom it will be known as "the mountain
of the Lord's house," from which the Lord is to rule
the world (Isa. 2:2-3). This lifting of the city and the
changing of the surrounding countryside into a
level plain are important to the fulfilling of another
prophecy. A river will spring from a subterranean
source at Jerusalem and flow in two directions:
westward toward the Mediterranean, and eastward
toward the Jordan valley and the Dead Sea (Zech.
14:8).

Several of the prophets speak of this new river
that beautifies and refreshes Palestine during the
Kingdom. Joel wrote, "A fountain shall come forth
of the house of the LORD, and shall water the valley
of Shittim" (Joel 3:18), the barren valley of the Jordan north of the Dead Sea. As the psalmist sang of
the glories of the Kingdom, he gave us the lovely
statement, "There is a river, the streams whereof
shall make glad the city of God, the holy place of
the tabernacles of the most High" (Ps. 46:4).

The most detailed description of the river is found
in Ezekiel (Ezek. 47:1-12). In his vision of the Kingdom the prophet was taken by an angel to the
sanctuary of God. Waters gushed eastward from
under the threshold of the temple. The angel led
Ezekiel through these waters, measuring them until
they had gone about a third of a mile. They were
ankle deep. In another third of a mile the water

reached his knees, and later they came to his loins. After the prophet had walked through the stream for a distance of a mile and one third, he wrote, "It was a river that I could not pass over: for the waters were risen, waters to swim in, a river that could not be passed over" (Ezek. 47:5). The word translated "risen" may be translated "increased," implying the existence of other springs along the course of the flow large enough to make it a navigable river.

Growing on both banks were many trees bearing fruit suitable for food, with leaves having medicinal properties "because their waters they issued out of the sanctuary" (Ezek. 47:12). The river flowed eastward into the desert, bringing life to the barren countryside. It finally emptied into the Dead Sea, making its water so fresh that it provided a home for a very great multitude of fish. Along the western coast of the Dead Sea was a fishing industry, from En-gedi at the middle of that coast to an unknown place called En-eglaim.

For the water of the Dead Sea to become fresh, there would have to be an outlet for the great new river flowing into it. The present topography of the land makes the natural outlet the one-hundred-mile stretch of dry valley reaching from the southern end of the Dead Sea to the Gulf of Aqaba along the Great Rift. This is confirmed by the use of the Hebrew word *Arabah,* translated "desert" in Ezekiel" 47:8. The dry valley below the Dead Sea is called the Arabah.

Ezekiel spoke of "the rivers" in Ezekiel 47:9. Rabbinical interpreters have generally understood this to mean that the new river has two branches, one going into the Mediterranean and one into the Dead

Sea. Such a flow, called for in prophecy and required by the geological formation of the land,
would make the Dead Sea the finest inland port in
the world, and it would be adjacent to Jerusalem.
The Mediterranean and the Indian Ocean would be
connected by way of this watercourse.

Another topographical change was mentioned by
Isaiah in connection with the establishing of Messiah's Kingdom. "And the LORD shall utterly destroy
the tongue of the Egyptian sea; and with his mighty
wind shall he shake his hand over the river, and shall
smite it in the seven streams, and make men go
over dryshod" (Isa. 11:15).

The tongue of the Egyptian Sea is understood to
be the Gulf of Suez. When this is destroyed the Suez
Canal will disappear. The new route for shipping
between the Mediterranean and the Indian Ocean
will pass through the land of Israel by way of its new
river. The Jewish people will have complete control
of commerce at the place where Europe, Asia, and
Africa meet, making Israel the most strategically
situated nation in the world.

Scripture usage makes it certain that the river
God will smite into seven streams is the Euphrates.
This prophecy is to be compared with another passage having to do with the same river in the latter
days. "And the sixth angel poured out his vial upon
the great river Euphrates; and the water thereof was
dried up, that the way of the kings of the east might
be prepared" (Rev. 16:12). Whether or not both
passages refer to the same divine act, something is
going to happen to this historic river in the end time,
changing it so that it is no longer a barrier to the

movement of people, as it has been through the centuries.

It should be mentioned that Ezekiel's great prophecy of the millennial river has often been spiritualized or allegorized. It has been insisted that this is not a real river at all, but a "spiritual river" depicting the flow of divine blessing from Jerusalem, deepening and widening as it flows. Whatever application may be made of this part of God's Word as an illustration of the blessing of God, there is nothing in the text to suggest that it is not a literal river of real water, with real trees growing on its banks, and actual fish, nets, marshes, and salt in the Dead Sea basin into which it flows.

Some critics have declared that the laws of nature would be violated by a river flowing from the elevated city of Jerusalem. It need only be pointed out that elementary books of physics carry diagrams showing how artesian wells can exist in places hundreds of miles from mountains. The underlying stratum carries water from the heights where it originates to the regions where it pours from the ground. People living near Death Valley are aware that springs are found there near mountain tops rather than in the valley. In Florida and elsewhere there are freshwater springs large enough to form navigable streams far from the source of the flow.

14

The Land in the Kingdom

In modern times geologists have discovered a
fault line in the earth's surface running through the
Persian Gulf and up the Euphrates valley. Eventually
it turns west to the Mediterranean, passing somewhere in the region of Hamath. This rift lies between
the Arabian plate of the earth's crust and the Eurasian plate. It is a major fracture zone where the
Arabian peninsula is pushing hard against the
Eurasian continent, and the source of frequent
earthquakes, particularly in Turkey and Iran.

The existence of a fault line separating the Arabian peninsula from the Eurasian continent is an
astonishing discovery in view of what may be the
borders of the land ultimately occupied by the
people of Israel during the Kingdom age. The
boundaries of the land are to be far more extensive
than they have been in the past. In a passage that
mentions the Tribulation and the resurrection as
well, Isaiah wrote, "Thou hast increased the nation,
O LORD, . . . Thou hast extended all the borders of
the land" (Isa. 26:15, NASB). The original borders

were named when God gave that part of the world
to Abram. He said, "Unto thy seed have I given this
land, from the river of Egypt unto the great river, the
river Euphrates" (Gen. 15:18; see also Deut. 1:7,
11:24; Josh. 1:4).

If the river of Egypt is the Nile, as many scholars
believe it is, then the two borders mentioned to
Abram correspond to the vicinity of the Great Rift
where it runs up the Red Sea parallel to the Nile,
and the fault line extending from the Persian Gulf
through the nearly eighteen hundred miles of the
Euphrates valley. These lines of cleavage make the
Arabian peninsula a region of the earth's surface
quite distinct from the Eurasian and African continents, and suggest the possibility that Israel is to
possess the entire peninsula in the Kingdom. The
Red Sea is mentioned as one border in Exodus
23:31. It has been suggested that "the east sea"
given as a limit of the land in Ezekiel 47:18 may
actually be the Persian Gulf, which is called "the
Eastern Sea" in contrast with the Mediterranean,
the western sea, on modern maps.

With the vast Syrian and Abraian deserts restored
to fertility in the kingdom, the peninsula could support the greatly increased numbers of the people of
Israel mentioned in prophecy (Deut. 30:5; Ezek.
37:26), as well as the Gentiles who are also to have
an inheritance in the land at that time (Ezek. 47:22).
The dimensions given by Ezekiel in connection with
the dividing of the land seem to require that the
distance between the Mediterranean and the Jordan River is to be greater after the cataclysmic
changes taking place at the Lord's return.

The borders of the land divided among the

people at the beginning of the Kingdom as described by Ezekiel are similar to the borders given at
the time the people entered Canaan under Joshua
(Num. 34:1-12; Josh. 15:1-12). In both cases the
area actually settled is much smaller than the area
God originally gave to His people. After the terrible
slaughter of the people during the Tribulation, their
numbers may be comparable to the size of the
company that came out of Egypt. The fact that limited strips of land between the Mediterranean and
the Jordan are marked off for the tribes to occupy
as the Kingdom is inaugurated does not mean they
will not afterward possess a much larger country as
they multiply during the Kingdom. They never occupied all the land God designated as their inheritance in Old Testament days, but He gave the larger
area to them for an everlasting possession. It will
surely be theirs under the Messiah's rule.

It is not surprising that after God has shaken the
heavens and the earth with the results described in
prophecy, extraordinary climatic changes that will
not affect the seasons will occur. "While the earth
remaineth, seedtime and harvest, and cold and
heat, and summer and winter, and day and night
shall not cease" (Gen. 8:22). The most striking
prophecy of this kind has to do with the sun and the
moon. "Moreover the light of the moon shall be as
the light of the sun, and the light of the sun shall be
sevenfold, as the light of seven days, in the day that
the LORD bindeth up the breach of his people, and
healeth the stroke of their wound" (Isa. 30:26). Although it is possible that this speaks of the limited
time during which God is restoring His people amid
violent upheavals, most commentators understand

it to refer to the kingdom age.

Harmful rays and unbearable heat would certainly be screened out more completely than they have been in a world under the curse. Crops would mature rapidly, producing great abundance. This is exactly what is predicted: "Behold, the days come, saith the LORD, that the plowman shall overtake the reaper, and the treader of grapes him that soweth seed; and the mountains shall drop sweet wine, and all the hills shall melt" (Amos 9:13; cf. Ps. 72:16). When the moon shines as brightly as the sun now does, it would appear that street lights will be a thing of the past, as will everything else needed to illuminate the darkness during the present age. The great increase in solar energy may be responsible for the great increase in human longevity, when men live to be as old as the trees.

Along with an increase of light, there will be an increase of rainfall in a land that has been parched for centuries (Ezek. 34:26). It is then that the familiar words will be fulfilled, "The desert shall rejoice, and blossom as the rose. . . . in the wilderness shall waters break out, and streams in the desert. . . . And the parched ground shall become a pool, and the thirsty land springs of water" (Isa. 35:1-7). Since these conditions will be normal for that age, they will come to be taken for granted, making it easy to understand why the former things will not be remembered (Isa. 43:18).

At that time God will speak to His land: "Behold, I am for you, and I will turn unto you, and ye shall be tilled and sown . . . and will do better unto you than at your beginnings" (Ezek. 36:9-11). He also will say

to His people, "Ye shall dwell in the land that I gave
to your fathers; and ye shall be my people, and I will
be your God" (Ezek. 36:28).

In this glorious golden age of the earth, lush vegetation will cover the deserts. "I will open rivers in
high places, and fountains in the midst of the valleys: I will make the wilderness a pool of water, and
the dry land springs of water. I will plant in the wilderness the cedar, and shittah tree, and the myrtle,
and the oil tree; I will set in the desert the fir tree,
and the pine, and the box tree together" (Isa.
41:18-19). The ending of the curse will transform the
land. "Instead of the thorn shall come up the fir tree,
and instead of the brier shall come up the myrtle tree:
and it shall be to the LORD for a name" (Isa. 55:13).
The astonished people will say, "This land that was
desolate is become like the garden of Eden" (Ezek.
36:35).

The face of the land is going to be changed by
the Lord, but human activity is also to have its part.
"They shall build the old wastes, they shall raise up
the former desolations, and they shall repair the
waste cities, the desolations of many generations"
(Isa. 61:4). "Men shall buy fields for money, and
subscribe evidences, and seal them, and take witnesses" (Jer. 32:44; see also 32:15). "And they shall
build houses, and inhabit them; and they shall plant
vineyards, and eat the fruit of them" (Isa. 65:21).
Private property will be respected, and people will
no longer be afraid. "They shall sit every man under
his vine and under his fig tree; and none shall make
them afraid; for the mouth of the LORD of hosts hath
spoken it" (Mic. 4:4). Nor will freedom from fear be
limited to certain safe areas. "They shall dwell safely

in the wilderness, and sleep in the woods" (Ezek. 34:25).

The prophets often dwell on the universal peace to be enjoyed during the Messiah's Kingdom (Isa. 9:6). He, the Prince of Peace, will make wars cease to the ends of the earth (Ps. 46:9). Doubtless the best-known prophecy of the coming of worldwide peace is, "They shall beat their swords into plowshares, and their spears into pruninghooks: nation shall not lift up sword against nation, neither shall they learn war any more" (Isa. 2:4; Mic. 4:3). Incidentally, this passage indicates the existence of industry in the Kingdom. In the absence of war and the manufacture of munitions and war material, the resources of the land will be used to improve human life and property rather than to destroy it.

Prophecy about conditions during the millennial Kingdom does not overlook the animal creation. God has promised to make a covenant with the beasts of the field, the fowls of heaven, and the creeping things of the ground (Hos. 2:18). Animal nature will be changed, and conditions will be restored to the way they were before sin entered the earth. One of the most famous of all prophetic passages is devoted to this theme.

> The wolf also shall dwell with the lamb, and the leopard shall lie down with the kid; and the calf and the young lion and the fatling together; and a little child shall lead them. And the cow and the bear shall feed; their young ones shall lie down together: and the lion shall eat straw like the ox. And the sucking child shall play on the hole of the asp, and the weaned child shall put his hand on the cockatrice's den. They shall not hurt nor destroy in all my

holy mountain: for the earth shall be full of the
knowledge of the LORD, as the waters cover the sea"
(Isa. 11:6-9).

When the land was divided among the tribes
under Joshua, he was told by the Lord, "Divide thou
it by lot unto the Israelites for an inheritance" (Josh.
13:6). Maps based on a careful study of the text
show an irregular distribution of ancient Palestine
among the various tribes.

The instructions given to Ezekiel are similar, with
the important distinction that the land is to be divided into what are evidently equal strips running
east and west. He was told, "Ye shall divide it by lot
for an inheritance unto you, and to the strangers
that sojourn among you: . . . they shall have inheritance with you among the tribes of Israel" (Ezek.
47:22).

When cartographers have tried to show what this
arrangement will look like, they have been in general agreement, but it should be understood that
the map accompanying these studies is intended
only to be suggestive. There are two or three points
about which students are not in agreement because
the text of Ezekiel, being necessarily brief, does not
supply every detail we might like to have. The size of
the portions given to each tribe is not specified. It is
deduced from a study of certain measurements,
and from landmarks mentioned in the text, where
these can be identified. It is assumed these will be
relatively unchanged after the geological distur-
bances taking place at the Lord's return.

One of the greatest difficulties in mapping the
divisions is uncertainty about the unit of measurement used by Ezekiel in giving the dimensions of

the portions of land given to the Levites, the priests, and the city. Cubits and reeds are both mentioned in the context. A cubit is eighteen inches; a reed is "six cubits long by the cubit and an hand breadth" (Ezek. 40:5).[1] The unit is not specified in most of the measurements. Some versions of the Bible insert one term, some the other. If the unit is intended to be the cubit in measurements of the city and the land, then the city in the Kingdom will be only two miles square. If the unit is the reed, then the city will be eleven miles square, a tremendous difference. On the attached map the larger dimension is used.

Beginning with Dan in the far north, portions of the land are to be given to each of seven tribes until Judah's portion is reached, evidently in the vicinity of the Sea of Galilee (Ezek. 48:1-7). The next two portions are set apart for the Levites and the priests. Then, just to the north of the great new river dividing the land into two parts, a strip perhaps eleven miles wide is to be given to the new city of Jerusalem, including its suburbs, with gardens as wide as the city itself on both sides providing produce for those who serve the city. A portion for "the prince" is at either end of the strip (Ezek. 48:8-22). It has been suggested that the prince may be David, raised from the dead, because of the statement made earlier, "My servant David shall be their prince for ever" (Ezek. 37:25; this view presents serious problems). Below the area containing the new city, portions of land are to be given to the remaining five tribes, beginning with Benjamin just south of the river and ending with Gad in the extreme south (Ezek. 48:23-29).

These strips of land are usually shown as extend-

ing from the coast of the Mediterranean eastward to
the vicinity of the Jordan. The text seems to show
this, but nothing is said about the division of the
remainder of the land promised to Abraham and his
descendants, which is extensive and probably very
much larger than what we think of as Palestine today. In the absence of any real knowledge of what
the land is going to be like in the Kingdom, maps of
its future divisions must be superimposed on maps
showing its boundaries as we know them today. It
must be remembered that in trying to picture what
Ezekiel described, we are seeking to map a land as
it will be after the worst earthquake in history, and
after such physical changes as will make the land
totally unrecognizable as the country commonly
called Palestine today.

The most outstanding feature of the land after
the Lord's return will certainly be the area of the
sanctuary and the new city, lifted high above the
plain to a place of extraordinary prominence. It will
be known as "the mountain of the LORD'S house"
(Isa. 2:2). At its peak will stand the sanctuary of the
Lord. Some eleven miles down the southern slope,
the glorious new city will overlook the river and the
plain. (Ezek. 40:2). A canopy of glory will crown the
mountain (Isa. 4:5). Palestine will have become the
glory of all lands (Ezek. 20:15), fulfilling the promise, "Ye shall be a delightsome land, saith the LORD
of hosts" (Mal. 3:12).

THE CITY OF JERUSALEM

15

A Remarkable City

Jerusalem has the most astonishing history of any city in the world. It goes back four thousand years, during which the world has witnessed the birth, growth, wealth, and power of many famous capitals. Some of these have become great commercial centers exerting tremendous influence, have developed a notable culture, and have accumulated great wealth. One by one they have declined and died or have been overthrown, destroyed, forsaken, or forgotten. Even their ruins have disappeared.

Meanwhile, Jerusalem has undergone at least twenty-seven sieges and has been completely destroyed, abandoned, and even ploughed like a field. Yet it has risen again and again from its ruins. The historian Milman in his *History of the Jews* wrote, "It might almost seem to be a place under a peculiar curse: it has probably witnessed a greater portion of human misery than any other spot under the sun."

The first reference to Jerusalem in the Bible is in

Genesis 14 under its ancient name, Salem, a word
meaning "peace." Abraham the patriarch was returning from a military victory over the group of
pagan kings who had invaded the country. He was
met by a mysterious character named Melchizedek,
king of Salem and priest of the most high God. The
king blessed the patriarch and received tithes from
him. Melchizedek marked the occasion by bringing
out bread and wine, the same elements used by
Jewish people in the passover and by Christians in
the Lord's Supper today (Gen. 14:17-20).

Here at the beginning of the revealed history of
Jerusalem we are given a glimpse of the city as it is
to be during the Kingdom age. For a moment we
see it as the center of a peaceful kingdom ruled by a
man whose name means "king of righteousness,"
and who is also king of Salem, that is, king of peace
(Ps. 110:4; Heb. 7:1-10). It is a picture of the future:
"Behold, a king shall reign in righteousness" (Isa.
32:1), whose name will be "The Prince of Peace"
(Isa. 9:6). Jerusalem is to be His capital (Jer. 3:17).
He will be a priest upon his throne (Zech. 6:13).
When the prophets describe Jerusalem as it is
going to be in the millennial age they say, "The king
of Israel, even the LORD, is in the midst of thee"
(Zeph. 3:15).   God chose one nation and one land
as peculiarly His own, but it is revealed that He also
chose a city. There are more than thirty references
to this fact. "I have chosen Jerusalem, that my
name might be there" (2 Chron. 6:6). "The LORD
hath chosen Zion; he hath desired it for his habitation" (Ps. 132:13). Furthermore, it is prophesied
that "the LORD . . . shall choose Jerusalem again"
(Zech. 2:12), when the time has come for Him to

intervene in human history by giving the reins of government to His Son.

Two other important revelations about the city must be put alongside these. "The LORD hath founded Zion" (Isa. 14:32), making this the only city in the world established by the Lord Himself. Again, "Thus saith the Lord GOD; This is Jerusalem: I have set it in the midst of the nations and countries that are round about her" (Ezek. 5:5). No one but God would dare to make such a statement. The sovereign God chose the spot on which His city was to stand, at the very center of the nations of the world. He designed the very crust of the earth in such a way as to bring about the geological changes He purposes in the day the Messiah comes to reign from Jerusalem, changes that will make this future world metropolis the joy of the whole earth.

The remarkable location of the city was better known in ancient times than it is today, when the content of the Word of God is neglected. A map hanging in the Hereford Cathedral in England shows the world as a circle, with Jerusalem at its very center. The map was prepared in A.D. 1280. The Marine Museum in Haifa displays a copy of *Itinerarium Sacrae Scripturae* containing a wood-cut by Heinrich Buenting dated 1581. It depicts the world as shaped somewhat like a three-leaf clover. The upper two petals are named Europa and Asia, and the lower petal, Africa. They join in the center at the city of Jerusalem.

Compared with other noted cities, Jerusalem is located in a strange place. Archaeologists and historians have wondered why it should have been established where it was, and why it should have become great. It has always stood on a remote spot, far removed from the main routes of commerce. It has no seaport or navigable river. Isolated by mountains and deserts, it stands on a rocky eminence with no water supply except for one modest spring. Very little productive soil is nearby. What are called the shepherds' fields are small. The area possesses no mineral riches. Every economic, agricultural, and topographic factor has always been against its ever becoming anything more than an unimportant little mountain town.

Yet Jerusalem has had a greater influence on the entire world than any other city, no matter how richly endowed or long enduring. Millions have cherished it as a holy city throughout many centuries. David and Solomon reigned there, and the great prophets spoke there. It is the only city ever to contain a temple in which the presence of God was manifested. In or near Jerusalem Jesus of Nazareth was crucified, buried, and raised from the dead. From that place He ascended to heaven, and to it He will return some day. The present age began when the Holy Spirit descended on the church at Jerusalem. That is where the gospel was first preached, the first martyrs were killed, and the first church council was held. Church history began there. The Crusades were an attempt to take the city from the Muslims. Against Jerusalem the nations of the world will some day be assembled in battle. After the Lord's return it will become the world metropolis as the prophecy is fulfilled, "I . . . will dwell in the midst of Jerusalem" (Zech. 8:3; see also 8:8).

Israel's capital city is mentioned some twelve

hundred times in the Bible under various names. The richest source of these is the book of Isaiah, where at least thirty names and titles are applied to it. It is called Zion, the city of David, the holy city, the city of the Lord, the city of righteousness, the mountain of the Lord's house, and My holy mountain Jerusalem.

The Bible teaching about Jerusalem is always factual and reasonable. It has repeatedly been confirmed by the findings of archaeologists. This is in contrast with widely held superstition. Visitors to the Church of the Holy Sepulchre are told Adam was formed of dust taken from what is now the city. For centuries some of this dust was displayed in the church. Here, it is claimed, Adam offered the first sacrifice, and here he was buried. Few tourists seem to be surprised to find his tomb displayed inside the church, untouched by the flood of Noah's day or the passage of time. It is conveniently located directly beneath the traditional site of Calvary. The claim is made that the blood of Jesus of Nazareth dripped down on Adam's skull, cleansing him and his descendants from sin. At this spot sacrifices are said to have been offered by Cain, Abel, Noah, and Abraham. Other traditions say the men of Jerusalem have always been more handsome, and its women more beautiful, than any others, and its water the purest and sweetest in the world.

In David's time, "the stronghold of Zion" stood on the top of a steep, rocky plateau covering a space of about eight acres. This seems small today, but it was normal for such fortresses in those days. Archaeology has shown the walled city of Megiddo covered fifteen acres, Gezer eighteen, and Beth-Shemesh, eight. Such places may be compared with the acropolis at Athens or the forts of early America. People living in the cultivated areas surrounding the stronghold could take refuge inside in times of war or danger. The outer, populated area was considered a part of the city.

The ancient hill of Zion was located south of the present walled city of Jerusalem, at some distance from what is now called the Dung Gate. It was shaped like a human foot. High walls enclosed it along the top of the steep, rocky scarps above the Kidron Valley to the east, the Tyropoeon valley to the west, and the valley of Hinnom to the south. On the slopes below the city, other walls were erected to protect houses built on terraces like those of the modern Arab town of Silwan, or Siloam, on the opposite side of the Kidron. To the north was a narrow saddle, or spur, of rock where three walls made defense easy.

Following the conquest of Canaan by the people of Israel, the stronghold of Zion remained in the possession of a pagan people called Jebusites for an astonishing four hundred years. It stood on the boundary between the tribes of Judah and Benjamin. The city itself was actually within the borders of Benjamin, but it was enclosed on two sides of the ridge by Judah. So impregnable was the site that neither tribe was able to take it. "As for the Jebusites the inhabitants of Jerusalem, the children of Judah could not drive them out" (Josh. 15:63). "The children of Benjamin did not drive out the Jebusites that inhabited Jerusalem" (Judg. 1:21). The reason was that the ridge on which it stood was very high and steep, with high walls at the crest. The Jebusites ridiculed any attempt by the Jews to take it. When David talked of capturing it the Jebusites boasted that even their blind and lame could defend it successfully (2 Sam. 5:6).

Perfectly situated for David's purpose to make it his capital city, the stronghold was centrally located among the tribes. If it had belonged either to Benjamin or Judah, there would have been jealousy on the part of other tribes after it became the capital. As it was, when David and his men captured it in approximately 1000 B.C., it became his own property, and he called it "the city of David." (This name was also given to Bethlehem, his birthplace, later on.)

How the ancient fortress fell is a fascinating story. The city's chief water supply was the spring Gihon (1 Kings 1:45), known today as the Virgin's Fountain, or The Spring of the Steps. Its water is now contaminated by seepage from the old, walled city.

The spring was located directly below the Jebusite city. Some one thousand years before David, a sixty-seven-foot tunnel had been cut through the rock into the cliff face under the city. It brought water from the spring to an underground pool. Above this, a forty-foot vertical shaft was cut from a tunnel that ran diagonally upward to a point inside the walls. Water containers were let down the shaft on ropes that passed through an iron ring that is still fastened to the ceiling above the place where an ancient platform stood. The Bible calls this water system "the gutter" in the King James Version, "the water tunnel" in the *New American Standard Bible* (2 Sam. 5:8). David challenged his men to climb the shaft. Joab succeeded, took the city by surprise, and was rewarded by being made chief of the armies of Israel (1 Chron. 11:5-6).

The old water shaft was discovered in 1867. In 1910 it was scaled by a British army officer without the use of ladders, duplicating Joab's feat. A number of other people have succeeded in making the same climb since then. Its discoverer, Captain Warren, for whom the shaft is named, considered its ascent so difficult that he was convinced Joab must have had an accomplice within the city. If so, Araunah the Jebusite could have been the man, because tradition says he was David's friend. He owned a threshing floor on the hill just north of the city of David, purchased afterward as the site of the temple. Near the bottom of Warren's shaft is the entrance to the conduit cut by Hezekiah to bring water from Gihon to the pool of Siloam in the city (2 Kings 20:20). Since the silt of many centuries has been cleared from Hezekiah's conduit, it is possible to walk through it today in water that may be waist deep.

Visitors today can hardly comprehend what the city was like in Old Testament days without knowing something of what has happened to it. It has been destroyed and rebuilt so many times that the accumulated rubble is from thirty to eighty feet deep beneath the present city. For example, to reach the old spring Gihon from the level of the road through the Kidron valley, one must descend thirty stone steps to reach the place where the water passes from the spring into the cavern in the side of Ophel.

Not only was the valley much lower in olden times than it is today, but the ridge on which stood the city of David was higher. According to Josephus, Simon

Maccabee, who died in 135 B.C. during the revolt against Syrian oppression,

> took the citadel of Jerusalem by siege, and cast it down to the ground, that it might not be any more a place of refuge to their enemies when they took it, to do them a mischief, as it had been till now. And when he had done this, he thought it their best way, and most for their advantage, to level the very mountain itself upon which the citadel happened to stand, that so the temple might be higher than it. And indeed, when he had called the multitude to an assembly, he persuaded them to have it so demolished . . . so they all set themselves to the work, and levelled the mountain, and in that work spent both day and night without any intermission, which cost them three whole years before it was removed, and brought to an entire level with the plain of the rest of the city. After which the temple was the highest of all the buildings, now the citadel, as well as the mountain whereon it stood, were demolished.[1]

This brought the western hill of Jerusalem to such prominence that it was erroneously believed later to be the ancient Zion, and is so called today. The valleys around the city are no longer as deep as they were, because Simon and others cast so much debris into them. However, as Josephus described the temple of his day, it was still very high above the surrounding valleys. He said of the royal cloister,

> For while the valley was very deep, and its bottom could not be seen, if you looked from above into the depth, this further vastly high elevation of the cloister stood upon that height, insomuch that if any one looked down from the top of the battlements, or down both those altitudes, he would be

giddy, while his sight could not reach to such an immense depth.[2]

In New Testament days the "pinnacle of the temple" was much higher than any spot in modern Jerusalem (Matt. 4:5-6).

Ophel, or the old city of David, is now a rather insignificant hill to the south of the walled city of Jerusalem. It is occupied by a number of pitiful Arab homes and is quite barren. Many tourists are unaware that the beautiful, ancient, walled city is modern compared with the city of David, and occupies a different site. Its walls were built in 1536 under Turkish sultan Suleiman the Magnificent. For the most part, they stand directly above the walls of the city that stood in New Testament times. An old Roman gate has been unearthed just beneath the Damascus gate.

16

Some Historical Notes

In 2 Kings 19:34 God states what may be regarded as a divine principle: "I will defend this city, to save it, for mine own sake, and for my servant David's sake." These words were given in connection with a particular incident, but they have often been illustrated in Jerusalem's past, and will find fulfillment again before the Kingdom dawns. Historically, the Lord has protected His city except when sin demanded that it be given over to the will of its enemies, as the prophets repeatedly warned.

The hand of God can be seen in the deliverance of Jerusalem from Absalom's attempt to wrest the throne from his father, David (2 Sam. 16-18), from the plague after David's sin of numbering the people (2 Sam. 24:15-16), and from the Assyrians under Sennacherib. On this latter occasion Hezekiah spread the defiant letter sent by his enemies before the Lord, prayed for help, and witnessed a remarkable, divine deliverance when the angel of the Lord went out and smote 185,000 Assyrian soldiers in one night with what was evidently a mysterious pestilence (2 Kings 19:14-15,35). After the city lay in ruins for many years following the exile, God raised up faithful men to restore and rebuild it. When Jerusalem becomes the center of a war involving all nations in the time of the end, it will please Him once again to save it from threatened total destruction (Zech. 14:1-3). Isaiah's words will be fulfilled: "So shall the LORD of hosts come down to fight for mount Zion, and for the hill thereof. As birds flying, so will the LORD of hosts defend Jerusalem; defending also he will deliver it; and passing over he will preserve it" (Isa. 31:4-5).

Even secular history is not without examples of what appears to have been supernatural activity in defense of the city. One of the outstanding examples was reported by the Jewish historian Josephus.[1] In the year 332 B.C. the soldiers of Alexander the Great moved across Palestine, intending to destroy Jerusalem. As the invading armies approached, Jaddua, the high priest, had a dream in which he was instructed to lead a procession of priests out from the city to meet the conqueror.

When Alexander met this procession, he astonished his generals by bowing to honor the God of Israel and embracing the high priest. The generals thought he had taken leave of his senses and questioned him. He told them he had seen a vision in Macedonia in which Jaddua appeared just as he was then, dressed in purple and scarlet, and followed by priests in white garments. The God of Israel had promised Alexander victory over the Persians if he spared Jerusalem.

After greeting Jaddua warmly, Alexander entered the city with him. There the high priest showed him the scroll of the prophet Daniel, where it was written that Greece, under the figure of a "rough goat," would indeed overcome the Medo-Persian empire. Alexander recognized himself in the words of the angel who spoke to Daniel: "The ram which thou sawest having two horns are the kings of Media and Persia. And the rough goat is the king of Grecia: and the great horn that is between his eyes is the first king" (Dan. 8:20-21). After the conqueror offered a sacrifice in the temple court, he granted the Jews liberty to live according to their own laws and freedom from taxes every seventh year.

The outstanding feature of the present walled city of Jerusalem is the Muslim *Haram ash Sharif*, or "noble sacred precinct." It is a great square dominated by the famous Dome of the Rock, or Mosque of Omar. The center of attention inside the Dome is an outcropping of rock, enclosed by a low fence of plate glass in bronze frames.

Tradition holds this place to be the spot where God sent Abraham to offer his son Isaac in sacrifice. The patriarch was directed to go to one of the mountains in the land of Moriah. When he reached the area, God directed him to a particular place. There Isaac was delivered from death when God provided a ram to die in his place (Gen. 22:1-14).

Students of the Word are deeply impressed by one particular detail in the record. Although the patriarch had been told to offer his son as a sacrifice to test his faith, he knew God had promised Isaac would have children. Therefore he knew his son would either be spared or be raised from the dead. He told his servants, "I and the lad will go yonder and worship, and come again to you" (Gen. 22:5).

The remarkable thing is that the form of the Hebrew in this sentence leaves no doubt that Abraham was sure both of them would be coming back. The New Testament comments on this. Abraham believed "God was able to raise him up, even from the dead; from whence also he received him in a figure" (Heb. 11:19).

Some eight hundred fifty years afterward, the place was owned by Araunah the Jebusite. He used it as a threshing floor, where the chaff was blown away from the wheat by the prevailing winds. On this high elevation just north of the stronghold of Zion, David was commanded by the Lord to set up an altar. The king bought the site and erected an altar there. God sent fire from heaven on his burnt offering. "Then David said, This is the house of the LORD God, and this is the altar of the burnt-offering for Israel" (1 Chron. 22:1).

At that place Solomon built his magnificent temple, "at Jerusalem in mount Moriah, where the LORD appeared unto David his father" (2 Chron. 3:1). Jewish tradition holds that all three of these incidents took place at the same place: the Moriah where Abraham was told to offer Isaac, the place where David built an altar at the Lord's command, and the Mount Moriah where the temple of Solomon was erected. It is the holiest of all places to the Jews.

When some three hundred fifty years later the people of Israel persisted in sin despite repeated warnings, Ezekiel prophesied, "Their holy places shall be defiled" (Ezek. 7:24). The most outstanding fulfillment of this word took place in A.D. 686, when the caliph Abd el-Malik, also called the caliph Omar, built the Dome of the Rock on the site of Solomon's temple. Doubtless this has preserved the sacred rock, but it is one of the holy places of Muhammadanism that no Jew has been permitted to enter. Surrounded by the largest court in the Near East, the mosque is one of the greatest sights in Palestine.

Five temples are mentioned in Scripture, all evidently erected at the same place. Solomon's temple was the first. It was destroyed by the armies of Babylon at the time of the captivity. After the Exile Zerubbabel erected another, which was completely rebuilt and enlarged by King Herod. This was the temple of New Testament days, put to the torch by the Roman armies in A.D. 70. A fourth temple is to be built by the people of Israel in the latter days. Because it certainly will occupy the same holy site revered by the Jews for centuries, students of prophecy expect to see the present Mosque of Omar destroyed some day, whether by earthquake, war, or some other cause.

There is no direct prophecy about the construction of such a temple, but several passages of Scripture refer to it. Daniel wrote of "the sacrifice and the oblation" (Dan. 9:27). Joel mentioned the porch and the altar (Joel 2:17). Christ warned of the abomination of desolation standing in the holy place (Matt. 24:15). The man of sin is going to sit in the temple of God (2 Thess. 2:4). John was told to measure the temple of God and the altar, and he was informed that the "court which is without the temple" was given to the Gentiles, who would tread it under foot forty-two months, understood to be the period of the Great Tribulation (Rev. 11:1-2).

The fifth and last temple at Jerusalem mentioned in Scripture is the millennial, or Kingdom, temple to be built by the Messiah. "Behold the man whose name is The BRANCH; and he shall grow up out of his place, and he shall build the temple of the LORD: even he shall build the temple of the LORD; and he shall bear the glory, and shall sit and rule upon his throne; and he shall be a priest upon his throne" (Zech. 6:12-13). The closing nine chapters of Ezekiel are largely given to a description of this temple and its worship.

The most striking similarity between Solomon's temple and the millennial temple is the presence of the glory of the Lord. This glory departed from the earth before Solomon's temple was destroyed but will return after the new temple is built. When the first temple was dedicated, "the fire came down from heaven, and consumed the burnt-offering and the sacrifices; and the glory of the LORD filled the house. And the priests could not enter into the house of the LORD, because the glory of the LORD had filled the LORD'S house" (2 Chron. 7:1-2).

In Ezekiel's vision of the millenial temple,

> behold, the glory of the God of Israel came from the way of the east: and his voice was like a noise of many waters: and the earth shined with his glory. . . . And the glory of the Lord came into the house by the way of the gate whose prospect is toward the east. So the spirit took me up, and brought me into the inner court; and, behold, the glory of the LORD filled the house (Ezek. 43:2-5).

The glory of the Solomonic temple was called the Shekinah by the Jews. The word comes from a root meaning "to dwell," or "to tabernacle." It referred to the fact that the glory was a manifestation of the presence of the Lord in their midst. It was a supernatural light, visible between the cherubim over the blood-sprinkled Mercy Seat of the Ark of the Covenant. This was in contrast with the pagan idolatry of the nations surrounding Israel, which required a visible image to worship. A remarkable thing about Ezekiel's vision is that the glory of the Lord is identified as a Person whose voice "was like a noise of many waters." That Person is the Messiah.

Ezekiel mentions the fact that in the Kingdom the glory is to enter the temple from the east, the same direction in which he was it leave in another vision. After the sins of the people had reached the point where God had to withdraw His presence from among them, the glory departed.

> Then the glory of the LORD went up from the cherub, and stood over the threshold of the house; and the house was filled with the cloud, and the court was full of the brightness of the LORD'S glory. . . . Then the glory of the LORD departed from off the threshold of the house, and stood over the cherubims. And the cherubims lifted up their wings, and mounted up from the earth in my sight. . . . and the glory of the God of Israel was over them above. . . . And the glory of the LORD went up from the midst of the city, and stood upon the mountain which is on the east side of the city (Ezek. 10:4,18-19; 11:23).

It is as though the Lord were reluctant to withdraw His presence from among His people, where it had dwelt ever since it first filled the tabernacle in the days of Moses (Exod. 40:34). Putting things chronologically, the glory went up from its place in the temple, stood for a time over the threshold, then moved away from the city to linger briefly over the Mount of Olives to the east. Finally it rose from the earth to disappear into the heavens, escorted by the cherubim.

There is a most interesting use of language in the New Testament that wonderfully complements the prophecy of Ezekiel. The Greek word *shekinize*, meaning "to dwell," is used of Jesus of Nazareth. "And the Word was made flesh, and dwelt among us, (and we beheld his glory) (John 1:14). The consonants of the Greek word rendered "dwelt" are identical with those of the Hebrew word *shekinah*.

The glory of the Lord is mentioned well over one hundred times in the New Testament. Its first appearance was at the incarnation, when shepherds were in the field at night. "And, lo, the angel of the Lord came upon them, and the glory of the Lord shone round about them: and they were sore afraid" (Luke 2:9). At the transfiguration He "was transfigured before them: and his face did shine as the sun, and his raiment was white as the light" (Matt. 17:2). The Lord is called "the brightness of his glory" in the book of Hebrews (Heb. 1:3), and "the Lord of glory" in James, a passage that reads in the margin, "the Lord the Glory" (James 2:1). It is noteworthy that the Lord ascended to heaven from the Mount of Olives and is to return to that mount, as both the Old and New Testaments declare (Zech. 14:3-4; Luke 24:51; Acts 1:9-12).

17

New Testament Prophecies

Jerusalem is mentioned nearly one hundred fifty times in the New Testament. The references are about evenly divided between the gospels and the book of Acts. There are ten altogether in the epistles, and four passages dealing with the new, heavenly Jerusalem. One of the most remarkable is the revelation that when Moses and Elijah appeared in glory with the Lord on the mount of transfiguration, they "spake of his decease which he should accomplish at Jerusalem" (Luke 9:30-31), suggesting that in heaven the earthly Jerusalem was a subject of keen interest.

New Testament prophecy about the city is of great importance, not only because it confirms Old Testament prophecy but also because it includes some passages that are demonstrably of divine origin. These stand on a par with Old Testament predictions that have been fulfilled with such remarkable accuracy that no enemy of the truth has ever succeeded in refuting them. Three of these outstanding passages are found in chapter 21 of the gospel of Luke.

When some of His followers spoke of the wonders of the temple, "how it was adorned with goodly stones and gifts, he said, As for these things which ye behold, the days will come, in the which there shall not be left one stone upon another, that shall not be thrown down" (Luke 21:5-6). Here was a statement so unlikely to be fulfilled that it must have sounded incredible. Word has come down to us of the temple's great beauty. Like a jewel in a beautiful setting, it dominated the great square crowning the top of Mount Moriah. Travelers approaching it from a distance commented that its white marble glistened like a mountain of snow. Against this background, fabulous amounts of gold shone in the sun. It was one of the most striking architectural monuments ever seen. When Titus, son of the emperor Vespasian, led the Roman armies against Jerusalem in A.D. 70, he was so impressed by the temple that he was determined such a gem must be preserved for posterity.

Titus gave orders that the temple was to be spared when the city was taken. Contrary to his wishes, it was set afire. It is not certain whether the Jews destroyed it to prevent its desecration by the enemy, or whether a soldier threw a lighted torch into it, as Josephus says. In a short time the tremendous structure was a mass of roaring flame. It burned for hours. When the ruins had cooled, the soldiers pried the stones apart and threw them down in an effort to recover the gold that had melted and run down through the cracks. The eagerness with which the soldiers tore the massive structure apart was also explained by a rumor to the effect that the Jews had buried a rich treasure somewhere in vaults underneath. The result was that not one stone remained upon another, as Christ had prophesied.

The great stones of the western wall, called the Wailing Wall for centuries because the Jews wept there for their departed glory and the loss of their temple, did not form a part of the temple itself. They formed the foundation for an outer wall at a considerable distance from the temple.

A second prophecy in this same chapter had to do with the destruction of the city and the escape of the Lord's followers.

> When ye shall see Jerusalem compassed with armies, then know that the desolation thereof is nigh. Then let them which are in Judaea flee to the mountains; and let them which are in the midst of it depart out; and let not them that are in the countries enter thereinto. For these be the days of vengeance, that all things which are written may be fulfilled (Luke 21:20-21).

If it should seem strange that the Lord told His followers to flee at a time when the city was completely surrounded by enemies intent on its destruction, the actual events explain it and demonstrate the perfect accuracy of the prophecy. A Roman general named Cestius led an army against the city some time before Titus came and destroyed Jerusalem. Cestius encamped on Mt. Scopus to the northeast, began his attack, and captured one wall and the suburb of Bezetha. Had he persisted in his effort, the city would have fallen quickly. Its people were ready to surrender, but a strange thing prevented it.

As Josephus tells the story, "It then happened that Cestius was not conscious either how the besieged despaired of success . . . and so he recalled his soldiers from the place, and by despairing of any expectation of taking it, without having received any disgrace, he retired from the city, without any reason in the world."[1] William Whiston, translator of Josephus, says in a footnote to this passage that the "Jewish Christians fled to the mountains of Perea, and escaped this destruction" that came later when the armies of Titus surrounded and desolated Jerusalem. As far as is known, not a single believer perished when the city was afterward destroyed. They had been waiting for the sign given by their Lord, strange though it may have seemed. Then one day the city was indeed compassed by armies. The sign had been given. When the armies mysteriously melted away, the followers of the Lord fled.

Philip Schaff wrote in his *History of the Christian Church*, "The Christians of Jerusalem, remembering the Lord's admonition, forsook the doomed city in good time and fled to the town of Pella in the Decapolis, beyond the Jordan. . . . An old tradition says that a divine voice or angel revealed to their leaders the duty of flight."[2] And well they might flee. One historian wrote that "A greater catastrophe than the mortal combat of the Jewish people with the Roman world power, and the destruction of the holy city, is unknown to the history of the world."

The legions of Titus brought to Jerusalem the horrors of famine, pestilence, and even cannibalism. The Roman soldiers executed the Jews without mercy as one part of the city after another fell into their hands. Over a million are said to have perished, and more than one hundred thousand were taken captive and sold into slavery. The population of Jerusalem had been greatly swelled by hundreds of thousands of Jews who flocked to the city for the Passover season, or who fled to it before the advancing armies.

History has recorded the astonishing accuracy with which every detail of these two prophecies was fulfilled. This fact must be remembered as we look at the third prophecy about the city found in Luke 21. "There shall be great distress in the land, and wrath upon this people. And they shall fall by the edge of the sword, and shall be led away captive into all nations: and Jerusalem shall be trodden down of the Gentiles, until the times of the Gentiles be fulfilled" (Luke 21:23-24). The first two-thirds of this prophecy has already been fulfilled. Distress did come to the land, dreadful beyond description. Wrath came upon the people of Israel. They fell by the edge of the swords of the Roman soldiers. Those who survived were led away captive into all nations, where their descendants are found today. Only the last two phrases of the prophecy about the city remained to be fulfilled. "Jerusalem shall be trodden down of the Gentiles, until the times of the Gentiles be fulfilled." No one can deny the historical fact that the city was under Gentile control for nineteen hundred years after these words were spoken, as it had been from the time of Nebuchadnezzar, some six-hundred years before Christ.

The important time word in the prophecy is "until," and the most difficult phrase to understand has to do with the fulfilling of the times of the Gentiles. The most widely held view of the meaning of Gen-

tile times is that the expression refers to the political
era during which no sovereign state of Israel existed.
It began when God withdrew sovereignty from Israel
and gave to Nebuchadnezzar the responsibility to
rule "wheresoever the children of men dwell" (Dan.
2:38). A similar statement is made about Cyrus,
king of Persia: "The LORD God of heaven hath given
me all the kingdoms of the earth" (Ezra 1:2). World
government has been in the hands of Gentiles ever
since about 602 B.C.

Inasmuch as the very letter of the Word has always been fulfilled in the past, it is important to take
note of the actual language used by the Lord here.
He indicated that the times of the Gentiles are some
day to be fulfilled. He did not say "ended," in this
particular passage. Some commentators have mistakenly assumed the two words are equivalent, with
the result that unwarranted statements have been
made about the end of Gentile times. For example,
when Jewish armies captured Jerusalem on June
11, 1967, it was recklessly claimed that this meant
the end of Gentile world government, but events
proved otherwise. Even before the city came under
Jewish control, some Bible students expected that
the end of the established order would come when
the rule of the city finally passed into Jewish hands.

The problem is greatly simplified if we give to the
word "fulfilled" the meaning it carries elsewhere. In
another place the Lord said, "The time is fulfilled,
and the kingdom of God is at hand" (Mark 1:15).
The time of which He spoke was the extended Old
Testament period during which the coming of the
kingdom was prophesied. That time had been fulfilled when He uttered these words, but it had not

ended. The Kingdom was "at hand," which may be rendered literally, "had drawn near." Had the people of Israel received Him as their Messiah, the Kingdom would soon have been established. When He was rejected, God introduced an entirely new age in which Gentiles were given the same privileges He accorded to the Jews of becoming members of the family of God through personal faith, or trust. The Kingdom that had been "at hand" was not established. It was revealed that it must await the completion of God's purpose for the present age.

Taking this meaning for the word "fulfilled," Luke 21:24 is easily understood. Just as the Kingdom was at hand when the time was fulfilled in Mark 1:15, something else will be at hand when the times of the Gentiles are fulfilled by the transfer of control of Jerusalem from Gentile to Jewish hands. The verses following this announcement inform us what is then at hand.

> And there shall be signs in the sun, and in the moon, and in the stars; and upon the earth distress of nations, with perplexity; the sea and the waves roaring; men's hearts failing them for fear, and for looking after those things which are coming on the earth: for the powers of heaven shall be shaken. And then shall they see the Son of man coming in a cloud with power and great glory. And when these things begin to come to pass, then look up, and lift up your heads; for your redemption draweth nigh (Luke 21:25-28).

Without attempting an exposition of these verses, it may be pointed out that whatever the heavenly signs are to be, the time when Jerusalem ceased to be trodden down of the Gentiles did coincide with

distress of nations and perplexity. People have been
fearing those things that are coming on the earth.
There is a widespread conviction that the end of the
world as we have known it may be at hand, that the
time is approaching when God will intervene in
human history.

No one can say how long a time must elapse
between the fulfilling of the times of the Gentiles
and their final end. Scripture is silent on this point.
Gentile times did not begin in one day. The Northern Kingdom of Israel fell in 721 B.C.; the Southern
Kingdom of Judah did not fall until 586 B.C., or 135
years later. Gentile times will not end until God's
moment has come. Then the prophecy will be fulfilled, "And in the days of these kings shall the God of
heaven set up a kingdom, which shall never be destroyed: and the kingdom shall not be left to other
people, but it shall break in pieces and consume all
these kingdoms, and it shall stand for ever" (Dan.
2:44). When we take Luke 21:24 literally, it seems to
be clear that the fall of Jerusalem to Jewish forces
in 1967 was an event of great importance. The
times of the Gentiles have evidently been fulfilled.
The last days of Gentile world rule must be upon us.
The sands in their hourglass are running out.

The history of the city of Jerusalem in the years
that have followed these words of the Lord are in
keeping with the position that we must take them
just as they stand. What He said became well known
throughout the Roman Empire. In the year A.D. 363
Julian the Apostate, emperor of Rome, determined
to prove Christ wrong by rebuilding the temple as
the center of a Jewish colony. He had been taught
the truth of Scripture but had turned his back on it.

He was convinced that if he could restore Jerusalem as the capital of the Jews while the power of the empire was at its height, he could show the Lord's prophecy to be false.

Therefore Julian encouraged the people of Israel to reconstruct their temple. They responded with enthusiasm. Wealthy Jews supported the undertaking by providing spades and pickaxes of silver. Rubbish was carried away in mantles of silk and purple. Suddenly an earthquake accompanied by "a whirlwind and a fiery eruption" scattered the temple foundations and terrified the workers. The project had to be abandoned. No one can claim this is folklore created by a superstitious people. The incident was recorded by historians of the day. The infidel Gibbon, in his *Decline and Fall of the Roman Empire*, quoted the famous pagan historian Ammianus Marcellinus regarding the mysterious occurrence. Then he made the comment, "Such authority should satisfy a believing, and must astonish an incredulous, mind," because the incident was attested "by contemporary and respectable evidence. . . . This praeternatural event was not disputed by the infidels."[3]

The power of the Roman Empire, supported by the wealth and enthusiasm of Jewish leaders, was unable to cause these words of the Lord to fall to the ground. The effort to prove prophecy wrong, even though initiated by the emperor himself, had to be given up. For centuries afterward the prophecy stood as a testimony to the accuracy of the Word and the folly of attempting to overthrow it. Jerusalem passed through a series of sieges, surrenders, famines, revolutions, restorations, and rebuildings. Constantine turned the city into a Christian shrine. Thereafter it changed hands frequently. It passed from the Persians to the Muslims, alternated between possession by the Crusaders and the Muslims, and then was taken by the Tartans, Egyptians, Mamelukes, Ottoman Turks, and British.

When the new state of Israel came into being in Tel Aviv on May 14, 1948, five Arab armies immediately invaded Palestine. The Jews were heavily outnumbered, but they astonished the world by winning one victory after another. Lacking any other explanation, the press began to speculate that God was fighting on the side of Israel. Bible students became convinced that momentous events were happening and looked forward eagerly to the fall of Jerusalem to the Jews.

Finally the armies of Israel approached the old, walled city. As they drew near and word of its capture was expected momentarily, suddenly the Jewish soldiers were halted just outside the Jaffa gate by the signing of an armistice. To the astonishment of those who had assumed prophecy was rapidly being fulfilled, Jerusalem remained under the control of Gentiles, that is, the Arabs. People who knew what the Lord said as recorded in Luke 21:24 rightly concluded that the time had not yet arrived for the times of the Gentiles to be fulfilled.

When in a whirlwind campaign the Jews took the old city away from the Arabs during the Six Day War, a dilemma faced those who had thought the end of Gentile control would bring the end of the times of the Gentiles. They finally concluded Jerusalem was still trodden down by the Gentiles, because the

Jewish leaders permitted its most sacred spot, the
temple site where the Dome of the Rock stands, to
remain in the hands of the Arabs. Another opinion
was expressed that this takeover was only temporary, "a mere military victory, of no prophetic significance." It was pointed out that the end of Gentile
times is not to come until after the Lord returns,
and it was claimed the Jewish victory had nothing to
do with Luke 21:24. These two opinions seem to
make the prophecy almost meaningless. Since the
days of confusion have passed, many have come to
take the literal view. Inasmuch as it is difficult to
maintain that the city is still trodden down by the
Gentiles, it is recognized by many students that the
times of the Gentiles must indeed have been fulfilled, that their end cannot be too far away, and that
we are living in days of tremendous importance
when God is preparing to restore sovereignty to His
ancient people.

18

Jerusalem in the Kingdom

Anyone who has read the Old Testament is aware of occasional statements about the earthly Jerusalem of the kingdom age, but the total revelation is likely to astonish even some Bible students. To get anything like a complete picture of what the city is going to be like after the Lord's return, it is necessary to examine what is written in at least eight Old Testament books. In some cases there is considerable information to be found in Hebrew roots and isolated texts.

For example, an obscure passage in Jeremiah settles the question of where the city is going to stand. "The city shall be builded upon her own heap" (Jer. 30:18). The word translated "heap" is the Hebrew *tel*, meaning a mound or hill made up of accumulated ruins. The Arabic *tel* is the source of our modern word *tell*, familiar in archaeology. It is an artificial mound built up of successive layers of debris where an ancient city has repeatedly been destroyed and rebuilt on the same site. In the Kingdom, Jerusalem will stand where it is now, above the ruins of the older cities that preceded it throughout history.

This is in agreement with other Scriptures. The Kidron is mentioned in connection with the city of the future, as are other geographic locations (Jer. 31:38-40). Ezekiel's statement that the Lord placed Jerusalem where it is, and Zechariah's revelation that it is to be elevated above the surrounding country, "and inhabited in her place," do not allow for the placing of the city at any other spot (Ezek. 5:5; Zech. 14:10). It is most interesting that when an attempt is made to map the land on the basis of its apportionment among the tribes, the present site of Jerusalem is found to lie within the borders of the new city. The great valley created at the Lord's return fits perfectly into the description of the bed of the river that is to flow east and west from Jerusalem in the Kingdom.

The prophet Ezekiel wrote, "In the visions of God he brought me into the land of Israel, and set me on a very high mountain; and on it to the south there was a structure like a city" (Ezek. 40:2, NASB). The mountain is "the mountain of the house of the Lord" on which Jerusalem stands, as the following chapters show, and the city is to be built on the southern slope. This is confirmed by the psalmist: "Beautiful for situation, the joy of the whole earth, is mount Zion, on the sides of the north, the city of the great King. God is known in her palaces for a refuge" (Ps. 48:2-3). The word "situation" here is better rendered "elevation," as it is in many versions of the Bible. It comes from a root meaning "wavelike," and "seems to denote a graceful wavelike height, not rugged and precipitous, but rising by a series of beautiful terraces."[1]

The expression "sides of the north" has given rise

to considerable speculation, having come down to us from about three thousand years ago, but it seems to mean only that the city of the great King is located on the flanks, or slopes, of the mountain that rises on the north side of the very great valley dividing Palestine into two parts after the Lord's return, and in which the millennial river flows.

Inasmuch as these "living waters shall go out from Jerusalem" (Zech. 14:8), it is hardly speculation to think of them as beautifying the city and the mountain by cascading down over the terraces and watering the luxurious vegetation that grows on the slopes. "The glory of Lebanon shall come unto thee, the fir tree, the pine tree, and the box together, to beautify the place of my sanctuary; and I will make the place of my feet glorious. . . . and they shall call thee, The city of the LORD, The Zion of the Holy One of Israel" (Isa. 60:13-14).

The millennial Psalms suggest something of the beauty of Jerusalem, as well as its general appearance. "Walk about Zion, and go round about her: tell the towers thereof. Mark ye well her bulwarks, consider her palaces; that ye may tell it to the generation following" (Ps. 48:12-13). These towers and palaces will be visible beyond the walls that strangers or foreigners are to build around the city, with gates that "shall be open continually; they shall not be shut day nor night" (Isa. 60:10-11). Ezekiel tells us there will be three gates on each side of the city, which is to be square, facing the four points of the compass. Each gate is to be named for one of the tribes of Israel; there will be twelve in all (Ezek. 48:31-34).

In size, Jerusalem will be about eleven miles

square, if the unit of measurement is the reed, which was some eleven feet long. Surrounding it are to be suburbs on each side, something over half a mile wide (Ezek. 48:17). This fact seems to support the view that the unit is the reed rather than the cubit, because the suburbs would be only half a city block wide if the cubit were used. Zechariah informs us that old men and women will sit in the streets of the city, among boys and girls playing there (Zech. 8:4-5). The Hebrew word rendered "streets" is literally "broad places," or "squares," making it a pleasant place of parks. It is going to be full of joy where is heard "the voice of joy, and the voice of gladness, the voice of the bridegroom, and the voice of the bride, the voice of them that shall say, Praise the LORD of hosts: for the LORD is good; for his mercy endureth for ever" (Jer. 33:10-11). Such an attitude toward the Lord will guarantee that there will be no divorces and no broken homes. Nor will illness cast a shadow over these families. "The inhabitant shall not say, I am sick" (Isa. 33:24).

Isaiah calls Jerusalem a quiet habitation. There will be no invading armies of "fierce people." The Hebrew text indicates that no ships of hostile invaders will ever be seen on its broad rivers and streams (Isa. 33:19-21, Hebrew text). The open gates of the city will look out on a peaceful and secure land in which there is nothing to make the people afraid. Flocks under the care of shepherds will be in the surrounding country (Jer. 33:13). The original language of Zechariah suggests the city will be inhabited as though it were open country where both men and cattle are found (Zech. 2:4-5). Poverty and decay will be so far removed that the Lord will bring gold to Jerusalem in place of brass, and silver in place of iron. Brass will be used in place of wood (Isa. 60:17-18).

Three very wonderful things will be true of Israel's capital during the Kingdom age. The Lord is going to dwell there, rule the earth from there, and receive the worship of the whole world in that holy mountain. He promised, "Lo, I come, and I will dwell in the midst of thee" (Zech. 2:10). The astonishing picture is given of the Lord rejoicing over the city with singing. "The Lord, is in the midst of thee. . . . The LORD thy God in the midst of thee is mighty; he will save, he will rejoice over thee with joy; he will rest in his love, he will joy over thee with singing" (Zeph. 3:15-17). This concept of a singing God is related to His residence there. "I am the LORD your God dwelling in Zion, my holy mountain" (Joel 3:17).

Furthermore, "the LORD of hosts shall reign in mount Zion, and in Jerusalem" (Isa. 24:23). "At that time they shall call Jerusalem the throne of the LORD; and all the nations shall be gathered unto it, to the name of the LORD, to Jerusalem" (Jer. 3:17). After that throne has been established, "many people shall go and say, Come ye, and let us go up to the mountain of the LORD, to the house of the God of Jacob; and he will teach us of his ways, and we will walk in his paths: for out of Zion shall go forth the law, and the word of the LORD from Jerusalem" (Isa. 2:3; see also Mic. 4:2).

The throne of the Lord will be the historic earthly throne of David. It is so called in Scripture: "Then Solomon sat on the throne of the LORD as king instead of David his father" (1 Chron. 29:23). In writing of the coming of the Prince of Peace, Isaiah said, "Of the increase of his government and peace there shall be no end, upon the throne of David, and upon his kingdom" (Isa. 9:7). Christians rejoice over the fact that this promise was repeated when the birth of Jesus of Nazareth was announced: "The Lord God shall give unto him the throne of his father David: and he shall reign over the house of Jacob for ever; and of his kingdom there shall be no end" (Luke 1:32-33).

There can be no mistake that it was Jerusalem of which the Lord spoke as "the place of my throne, and the place of the soles of my feet, where I will dwell in the midst of the children of Israel for ever" (Ezek. 43:7). It will stand in the sanctuary, the house of the Lord, considered a part of the city although it will be located north of the city proper, where "upon the top of the mountain the whole limit thereof round about shall be most holy" (Ezek. 43:12).

This King "shall reign in righteousness, and princes shall rule in judgment" (Isa. 32:1). "He shall judge among many people, and rebuke strong nations afar off" (Mic. 4:3). Whenever there is any resistance to His righteous rule, He will sternly use a rod of iron (Rev. 12:5). Some among the people born during the kingdom age will be unregenrate, wanting their own way and rendering only pretended obedience. Absolute justice and holiness will characterize His reign. He will sit on "the throne of his holiness" (Ps. 47:8), "a priest upon his throne" (Zech. 6:13). "Jerusalem shall be called a city of truth; and the mountain of the LORD of hosts the holy mountain" (Zech. 8:3). No city in history has ever earned such a name; untruthfulness and corruption are taken for granted in municipal govern-

ment. Jerusalem will take a new name from the fact
of the divine residence: "The name of the city from
that day shall be, The LORD is there" (Ezek. 48:35).
This name in the Hebrew is, "Jehovah-shammah."

More details about the city and sanctuary as the
center of world worship are revealed in the last nine
chapters of Ezekiel than anywhere else. An area of
the land about fifty miles square is set apart for holy
purposes. It will be divided into three parts. The
northern section will belong to the Levites, and the
southern section will contain the city, its gardens,
and the portion for the prince. In the center of the
central section given to the priests will stand the
altar, in front of the sanctuary. Around it will be a
vast square, one mile on each side, surrounded by
walls, with another enclosure inside this one, half a
mile square.

The tremendous size of the entire "oblation," or
allotment set apart for the Lord, is necessary because worshipers will come from all over the world
to this place. Provision is even made for control of
the traffic of the people who come. Those who
enter by way of the north gate in the wall must go
out by way of the south gate, whereas those who
come in from the south leave from the north (Ezek.
46:9). There will be no confusion caused by people
milling around. Such crowds will have to be fed;
there is a passage in Isaiah that may refer to it: "In
this mountain shall the LORD of hosts make unto all
people a feast of fat things, a feast of wines on the
lees" (Isa. 25:6).

No temple like this has ever yet been built. There
are some similarities to Solomon's temple, but
great differences as well. There is no reference to

the Ark of the Covenant. No high priest is mentioned; the Lord Himself will be present. The priests are of the family of Zadok, "that kept the charge of my sanctuary when the children of Israel went astray from me, they shall come near to me to minister unto me, and they shall stand before me" (Ezek. 44:15; see also 1 Sam. 2:35). They will teach, judge, and oversee the sacred feasts.

It is usually assumed that the river of Ezekiel 47, beginning at the sanctuary and growing wider and deeper as it flows, is the only stream associated with Jerusalem, but this may not be so. "There shall be upon every high mountain, and upon every high hill, rivers and streams of waters" (Isa. 30:25). The city will be a place of broad rivers and streams (Isa. 33:21). If students of the Bible err in their efforts to describe this future glorious city where the Creator of the universe will be pleased to reside, they err in the direction of understatement, because the revelation we have been given is very brief. Human language is not adequate to describe the wonder and beauty of the world metropolis as it will be during earth's golden age.

Nowhere is this more true than in Isaiah's tantalizingly short statement about a final detail found nowhere else. "Then the LORD will create over the whole area of Mount Zion and over her assemblies a cloud by day, even smoke, and the brightness of a flaming fire by night; for over all the glory will be a canopy" (Isa. 4:5; NASB). There in the very center of the earth, crowning its most delightful land, will stand God's holy mountain, surmounted by the loveliest structures ever seen by human eyes. On the southern slope the millennial city will rear its towers

and palaces above its shining walls. Crystal waters
will cascade down over its terraces to water vegetation more beautiful than has graced the earth since
Eden, because it will be untouched by the curse. At
the crest of the mountain will stand the sanctuary of
the Lord, surpassing the power of the pen to describe it. What does it mean, for example, when the
Lord says, "I will glorify the house of my glory" (Isa.
60:7)?

We know His glory was "like devouring fire on the
top of the mount in the eyes of the children of Israel" (Exod. 24:17) when they were in the wilderness. To Ezekiel it was as "a fire infolding itself"
(Ezek. 1:4), and it had "the appearance of the bow
that is in the cloud in the day of rain. . . . This was
the appearance of the likeness of the glory of the
LORD." (Ezek. 1:28). The glory of God will fill the
house, and over all the glory will be a canopy, reminding some of the wedding canopy over the
bride and groom at a Jewish wedding, because "as
the bridegroom rejoiceth over the bride, so shall thy
God rejoice over thee" (Isa. 62:5; see also Hos.
2:19-20).

The canopy is something the Lord will create for
the new age, covering all of Mount Zion, protecting
it and sanctifying it in the eyes of all beholders. It will
be seen as a bright cloud by day, and a flaming fire
by night. God, who went before His people in the
wilderness in a pillar of cloud and fire during the
years of their wanderings (Exod. 13:21), will again
cover His glorious mountain and all Israel's assemblies with a cloud and fire after they have entered their rest, and the city of the great King has
become the joy for the whole earth.

Notes

Chapter 14

1. Merrill F. Unger, *Unger's Bible Dictionary* (Chicago: Moody, 1966), p. 720.

Chapter 15

1. Josephus *Antiquities of the Jews* 13.6.7.
2. Josephus *Antiquities of the Jews* 15.11.5.

Chapter 16

1. Josephus *Antiquities of the Jews* 11.8.4-5.

Chapter 17

1. Josephus *Wars of the Jews* 2.19.7.
2. Philip Schaff, *History of the Christian Church,* 8 vols. (New York: Scribner's, 1882), 1:402.
3. Edward Gibbon, *Decline and Fall of the Roman Empire,* 6 vols. (Philadelphia: Lippincott, 1867), 2:435-40.

Chapter 18

1. F. C. Cook, ed., *The Bible Commentary,* 11 vols. (London: John Murray, 1882), 4:280.

Palestine, the Navel of the Earth,
Center of Earth's Land Mass

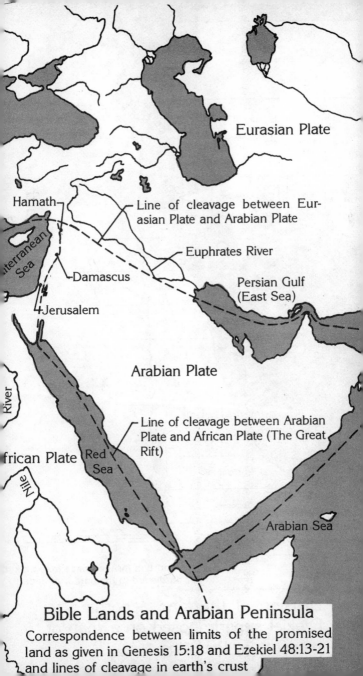

Eurasian Plate

Hamath — Line of cleavage between Eurasian Plate and Arabian Plate

Euphrates River

...terranean Sea

— Damascus

Persian Gulf (East Sea)

+ Jerusalem

Arabian Plate

— Line of cleavage between Arabian Plate and African Plate (The Great Rift)

River

frican Plate   Red Sea

Nile

Arabian Sea

Bible Lands and Arabian Peninsula

Correspondence between limits of the promised land as given in Genesis 15:18 and Ezekiel 48:13-21 and lines of cleavage in earth's crust

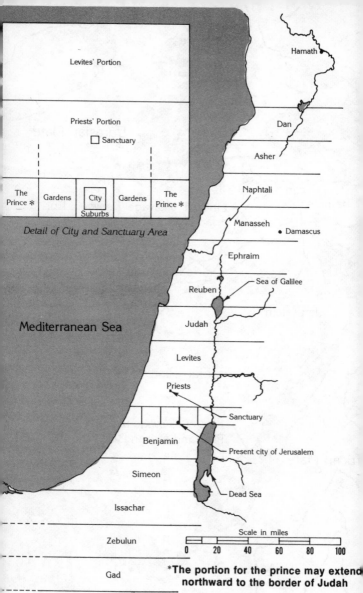

Detail of City and Sanctuary Area

Levites' Portion

Priests' Portion

□ Sanctuary

The Prince *

Gardens

City
Suburbs

Gardens

The Prince *

Mediterranean Sea

Hamath

Dan

Asher

Naphtali

Manasseh ● Damascus

Ephraim

Reuben — Sea of Galilee

Judah

Levites

Priests

Sanctuary

Benjamin

Present city of Jerusalem

Simeon

Dead Sea

Issachar

Zebulun

Scale in miles
0   20   40   60   80   100

Gad

*The portion for the prince may extend
northward to the border of Judah

Division of the land according to
Ezekiel superimposed on a map of
present-day Palestine

JERUSALEM

Woodcut map by Heinrich Buenting
Itinerarium Sacrae Scripturae
Helmstadt, 1581, Marine Museum, Haifa

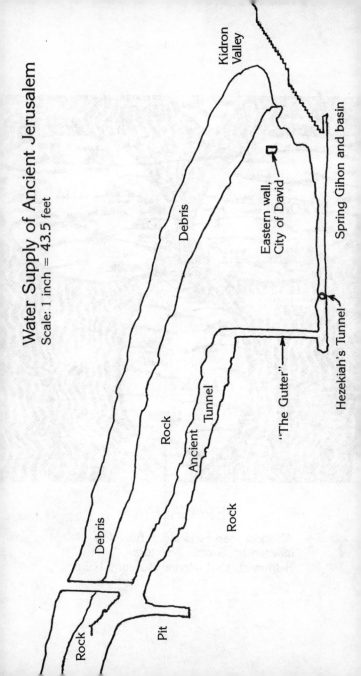

Water Supply of Ancient Jerusalem
Scale: 1 inch = 43.5 feet

Kidron Valley

Debris

Rock

Debris

Eastern wall, City of David

Ancient Tunnel

"The Gutter"

Rock

Rock

Pit

Spring Gihon and basin

Hezekiah's Tunnel

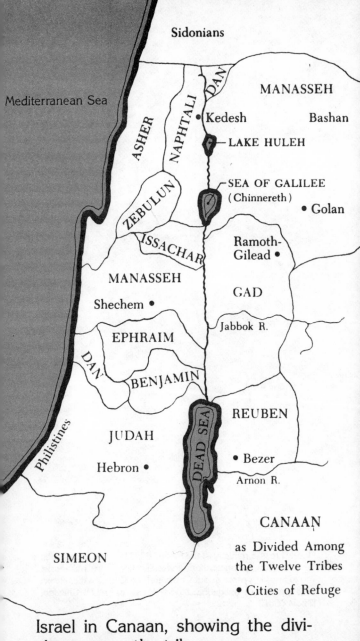

Israel in Canaan, showing the division among the tribes

- now - church age
- rapture
(after the elect or church are
chosen by God Jews & Gentile

1000 yr. reign - peace

judgement & destruction